To Jill
an inspiration as always!

love Larry

The Business Leader's Guide to the Low-carbon Economy

To Monica, Sorcha and Ró.

The Business Leader's Guide to the Low-carbon Economy

LARRY REYNOLDS

GOWER

Published by
Gower Publishing Limited
Wey Court East
Union Road
Farnham
Surrey, GU9 7PT
England

Gower Publishing Company
Suite 420
101 Cherry Street
Burlington,
VT 05401-4405
USA

www.gowerpublishing.com

British Library Cataloguing in Publication Data
Reynolds, Larry.
     The business leader's guide to the low carbon economy.
     1. Industries – Environmental aspects. 2. Industries – Energy conservation. 3. Carbon dioxide mitigation. 4. Carbon dioxide mitigation – Forecasting. 5. Renewable energy sources – Economic aspects. 6. Social responsibility of business.
     I. Title
     658.4'083-dc23

Library of Congress Cataloging-in-Publication Data
Reynolds, Larry.
     The business leader's guide to the low carbon economy / by Larry Reynolds.
          p. cm.
     Includes bibliographical references and index.
     ISBN 978-1-4094-2351-5 (alk. paper) – ISBN 978-1-4094-2352-2 (ebook)
     1. Business enterprises – Environmental aspects. 2. Management – Environmental aspects.
     3. Technological innovations – Environmental aspects. 4. Sustainability. I. Title.

     HD30.255.R49 2012
     658.4'083 – dc23

                                                                                          2012011067
ISBN 9781409423515 (hbk)
ISBN 9781409423522 (ebk – PDF)
ISBN 9781409471271 (ebk – ePUB)

Printed and bound in Great Britain by the
MPG Books Group, UK

Contents

About the Author

Larry Reynolds is Managing Partner of 21st Century Leader.

His company provides interactive live events and online resources to help business leaders face up to the challenges of leading in the twenty-first century. One of the greatest of these challenges is to create genuinely sustainable organisations fit for the low-carbon economy. Recent clients include The Co-operative Group, Renault and Tetra Pak.

Larry teaches leaders how to lead more effectively and facilitates organisational change. He also contributes to a wide range of free leadership resources that are available at www.21stcenturyleader.co.uk

Larry's live events are characterised by his energy and enthusiasm, his down-to-earth and jargon-free approach to leadership, and his determination to equip people with practical skills and knowledge that will really help them to be better agents of change.

Larry is the author of many books and articles on leadership and change, including *The Trust Effect*, *The Twenty First Century Leader*, and *Leading Change in Turbulent Times*.

Larry lives in Yorkshire with his wife and two daughters, who give him a greater sense of fulfilment than he can possibly express. An obsessive learner, only the invention of e-books and a desire for neatness and efficiency has saved Larry's house from being completely overwhelmed by books.

Acknowledgements

Many thanks to everyone who gave time and expertise to help with this book, especially: Mike Berners-Lee, John Broderick, Steve Brown, Russ Comrie, Anthony Day, Dave Dunbar, Nigel Holden, Clare King, Lucy Martins, Paul Monaghan, James Murray, Joanne Pollard, Charlie Rea, Louise Yates, and Haydn Young.

Introduction

During the next hour, the world will meet its energy needs by burning about a million tonnes of coal, 400 million cubic metres of gas and 4 million barrels of oil. This is in many ways a good thing. Cheap energy from fossil fuels not only kick-started the Industrial Revolution two hundred years ago, but enables many of us to live a life of luxury unimaginable to most kings and emperors throughout history. Your business – whatever it is – relies on cheap energy to make its contribution to that wonderful lifestyle we enjoy in the early twenty-first century.

Wonderful though fossil fuels are, they won't last for ever. This is partly because supplies are finite, and partly because burning them contributes to global warming. Because most governments around the world believe global warming is, on balance, a bad thing, they are making it more expensive and difficult for businesses to rely on cheap fossil fuel energy.

This creates both threats and opportunities. If you continue to use energy in the profligate way you used to when it was very cheap, you will soon be overtaken by more energy-efficient competitors. But if you go beyond mere energy-efficiency and create an organisation that can thrive in this new low-carbon economy, the decline of fossil fuels can create tremendous opportunities for you and your business.

The British TV show *Dragons' Den* gives entrepreneurs a chance to pitch ideas to potential investors – the dragons of the programme's title. These dragons take a lot of convincing to part with their cash: few of the entrepreneurs who appear receive even a single offer of funding. But something very unusual happened in the July 2011 show which opened the programme's ninth series: Yorkshire-based businessman Chris Hopkins received offers from no less than four of the dragons. After some tense negotiations, he walked away with a £120,000 investment.

Chris Hopkins's company isn't particularly unique or innovative: it installs solar panels. Solar photovoltaic (PV) panels have been around for more than fifty years, so what makes them such an attractive investment right now? Three factors have come together to make this company a dragon's dream: rising energy prices, an increasing awareness of environmental issues, and government incentives for renewable energy. Welcome to the low-carbon economy.

As energy prices continue to rise, as the effects of climate change become more tangible, and as government policies on energy develop and change, the economy itself will start to feel different. This new economy won't just affect Chris Hopkins and his millionaire investors; it will have implications for every kind of business.

At the other end of the scale from Chris Hopkins' small enterprise is retail giant Marks & Spencer (M&S). With 78,000 employees and a turnover of almost £10 billion, it is one of the UK's more successful retailers. In 2007 Chief Executive Stuart Rose launched Plan A, a five-year commitment to make the company more energy-efficient, reduce its carbon footprint, and generally become more environmentally friendly. By 2010 the company had met many of its initial targets, and in the words of Stuart Rose: 'We have proved you can be a sustainable ethical business and you can be more profitable by doing so.'

M&S is now working on its 2010–2015 targets, with the eventual aim of becoming the world's most sustainable major retailer.

But if you are looking towards the UK for a role model of a successful low-carbon business, you are probably looking in the wrong direction. With its turnover of $135 billion, Korean giant Samsung is currently one of the world's most successful consumer electronics firms. Ten years ago, when the company turned over $23 billion making batteries, industry experts were astounded at its ambition to become a major electronics firm in its own right. It achieved that goal in less than eight years. It recently announced its focus for the next ten years: solar panels, LED lights, electric vehicles, medical devices and biotech drugs. Just as electronics defined much of the late twentieth century, Samsung believes that the low-carbon economy will define much of the early twenty-first.

Almost all of the world's largest companies are taking the low-carbon economy very seriously. Most have ambitious plans to reduce energy usage, minimise their carbon footprint and increase resource efficiency. More than three quarters of the Fortune 500 companies already measure their operational carbon footprint in readiness for likely future mandatory carbon reporting. Some are investigating radically different business models in readiness for a new low-carbon world where long-term sustainability is as important as short-term profit.

Whether your company is large or small, whether you are in manufacturing, services or retail, the low-carbon economy will affect you and your business.

But just what will the effects be? Will energy prices level off, or will they continue to rise at ever-increasing rates? Is climate change really happening, and if so, how severe will its impact be on everyday life? How will your business be affected as we move from carbon-based fuels to renewables and nuclear? How quickly will electric cars displace the internal combustion engine? How soon will your customers start to care about the carbon footprint of your services and products? Is it either possible or desirable to be carbon-neutral as a company? What new products and services must your company provide in order to stay competitive?

This book will answer your questions about the low-carbon economy. It will tell you why the low-carbon economy is happening, and what it means in practice. More importantly, it will identify the opportunities the low-carbon economy offers your business and the practical steps you can take to make the best of these opportunities.

PART I

The Drivers of the Low-carbon Economy

On 10 March 1776 an unnamed engineer pulled a lever on a strange contraption on the outskirts of Birmingham. As steam entered the device's orifices and chambers, wheels began to turn and a gush of water showed that the machine was doing what it had been designed to do – pump water out of a mine shaft. The machine was the first of a new kind of steam engine designed by James Watt and Matthew Boulton. As well as firing the starting gun for the Industrial Revolution, Boulton and Watt were also unleashing a new kind of economy: an economy based on energy from hydrocarbons – coal, oil and gas.

For more than two hundred years the hydrocarbon economy has served us well. Today it enables most of the 7 billion people alive to enjoy a standard of life beyond the wildest dreams of the billion people alive in Boulton and Watt's day.

There are just two problems. Firstly, as supplies of coal, oil and gas decline and population increases, the price of fossil fuels can only rise, making them increasingly unaffordable. Secondly, even if we could afford them, burning fossil fuels is a major contributor to climate change. If climate change continues unabated, the consequences for life on Earth could be very bad. As a result, we're moving towards a different kind of economy: one that relies much less on fossil fuels, and much more on low-carbon alternatives. Most of this book is about what such an economy will be like, and the consequences for your business. But first, it's important to understand just how the twin forces of rising energy prices and climate change will drive the low-carbon economy.

1

The Cost of Energy

The days of cheap and easy oil are over.
Fatih Birol, Chief Economist, International Energy Agency

Every day you travel to work, three small miracles occur.

If you drive to work in a conventional vehicle, your journey is made possible only by oil. This oil was originally extracted from miles below the land or seabed, transported to a refinery where it was turned into usable fuel, and then transported by pipes, ships and trucks to your local petrol station. Cheap oil not only powers your car, it makes the manufacture of your car possible in the first place. The energy required to mine the metals, produce the plastics, assemble the parts and ship them from factory to forecourt all depends on oil. Indeed, it's cheap, oil-based transport that makes global trade possible.

Miracle number two is that you arrive at work to a pleasantly warm office, probably heated by gas. This too has travelled thousands of miles to get to you, possibly by pipeline from Norway or Russia, or by supertanker from the Middle East (a tiny trickle still comes from the North Sea, but this is declining fast). As well as heating your office, and possibly your home, gas is also an essential component in the production of nitrogen-based fertilisers that will have been used in the production of most of what you will eat today.

The final miracle occurs when you flick a switch to turn on your computer. Electricity surges from a power station far away, through the grid, at exactly the right frequency and voltage to boot up your computer and allow you to waste so much time dealing with emails. Nuclear power and renewables generate a little of this electricity, and a third of it is from gas, but the biggest single source of electricity in the UK still comes from burning coal. And of course, electricity doesn't just power your computer: it powers just about everything else in offices factories and homes that aren't heated by gas or propelled by oil.

Three fossil fuels – oil, gas and coal – currently supply most of the world's energy needs. The explosion in population, technology and living standards that has occurred on this planet in the last two hundred years since the Industrial Revolution has been possible only because these three fuels have been abundant and cheap.

The good news is that they're still abundant. There's enough oil, gas and coal buried below the surface of this planet for us to continue in this high-powered lifestyle for hundreds of years. The bad news is that they're no longer cheap. That's because we've already used up all the easy-to-get stuff. From now on, especially as far as oil and gas are concerned, getting it out of the ground is going to be extremely difficult – technically, politically and economically. This means that fossil fuels are likely to become very expensive indeed. This is mixed news for business. On the downside, all businesses use energy, and rising energy costs will hit your bottom line. On the plus side, you can gain considerable competitive advantage if you figure out ways to make your business more frugal with energy, or are able to develop appropriate products and services for a world where energy is much more expensive. We'll explore these opportunities in depth in Chapters 11–15. First, let's consider why energy costs will rise, by how much, and how quickly.

Oil

Most of the oil we used in the twentieth century was recovered from wells on land (in places such as Texas, Saudi Arabia and most of the Middle East) or in relatively shallow offshore waters (such as the North Sea). This kind of oil is cheap and easy to produce – less than $10 a barrel for some US oil fields.

When you first drill into any oil reservoir, the black gold comes gushing out. Recovering the oil from a newly drilled reservoir is easy – it just spurts out by itself. After a while, though, the pressure within the reservoir starts to fall, and the oil stops flowing. In order to build up the pressure again, you have to pump something back into the reservoir. Different methods are used, but pumping water in is fairly common. Maintaining the pressure in this way means you can maintain production for many years, but it will eventually tail off. At some point it becomes too expensive and difficult to extract any more oil, and the field is abandoned, even though perhaps a quarter of the oil is still down there.

The typical production pattern for a single field follows a bell-shaped curve – modest beginnings, a peak in production levels halfway through the life of the field, and tailing off towards the end. The exact shape of this curve depends on the size of the field and the amount of effort put into extraction. The UK's North Sea oilfields began production in 1975, peaked in 1999 at 6 million barrels per day (mbpd; a barrel of oil is about 160 litres) and are now steadily declining. In 2010 they produced around 4mbpd, and it's expected that output will be down to 3mbpd by 2020, and dry up some time in the 2030s.

In the 1950s a geologist at Shell called M. King Hubbert realised that this characteristic peaking of an individual oilfield could also be applied to all the oilfields in a particular region. In 1956 he predicted that the peak of crude oil production in the USA would occur between 1966 and 1972. Nearly all the experts at the time dismissed his prediction. The prevailing wisdom among the oilmen was: 'If we need more oil, we'll just drill for it!' But Hubbert's thinking was sound. US oil production did indeed peak in 1970, and has been declining ever since.

What applies to a country or region can also apply to the whole world. Using a similar methodology to Hubbert's, it's now generally accepted that supplies of conventional oil worldwide will peak some time soon, and decline thereafter.

The big question is: when? At what date will half the world's supplies of conventional oil be exhausted? Nobody knows for sure, partly because some of the people who own conventional oilfields are quite wary about sharing information about how much is left. Currently, almost an eighth of all the oil in the world comes from one huge field called Ghawar, in Saudi Arabia, and the rulers of that kingdom aren't saying how much is left. Nevertheless, quite a few people have had a go at predicting the peak. An industry specialist called Matt Simmonds did some phenomenally clever research based on data he was able to wheedle out of the Middle Eastern oilfields, and he reckons the peak will be in 2015. The UK has its very own Taskforce on Peak Oil and Energy Security, with membership drawn from companies in the transport, construction and energy industries. It reckons 2013 is the date. Its 2010 report predicts an energy crunch similar to the credit crunch within five years if the country fails to address energy issues urgently.

Even five years ago, the peak oil theory, as it was known, was quite controversial. At that stage it was a few environmentalists and an even smaller minority of oil industry experts who claimed that once oil supplies had peaked, energy prices would skyrocket and the world's economy would crash. Fast-forward to 2012 and everything has changed. For a start, the world's economy has crashed anyway, as a result of the 2008–2009 economic crisis. And almost everyone, from the big oil companies to the highly respectable and conservative International Energy Agency, now accepts that conventional oil is peaking around now, give or take a year or two.

If conventional oil – that is, oil extracted from land or shallow seas – were all we had, the world would already be facing a huge energy crisis. But we also have unconventional sources of oil – in deep waters, in tar sands and in oil shale.

DEEP WATER

If you are willing and able to drill in deep water, vast quantities of oil become available. What's stopping us? The first problem is sheer technical difficulty. It's one thing drilling 2 kilometres below the surface of the North Sea from a static platform: it's quite another to drill 5 kilometres below the seabed from a floating platform. As the 2010 failure of BP's Deepwater Horizon rig demonstrated, when things go wrong, they're very hard to fix in such testing environments. Deepwater drilling is also politically sensitive. Many people don't want to see drilling for oil in places like the Arctic, and those objections are multiplied when a disaster like BP's failure in the Gulf of Mexico causes widespread environmental damage.

Technical and political difficulties add to the cost. While a barrel of onshore oil might be produced for less than $10 a barrel, most estimates put the cost of a barrel of oil from the Arctic at over $100 a barrel. This isn't a problem if people are willing to pay the price. But there's a more fundamental limiting factor known by the acronym EROEI – Energy Return On Energy Invested. Producing energy – in the form of crude oil or anything else – requires energy. A land-based oil well might take one unit of energy to produce anything from 25 to 100 barrels of energy, an EROEI of 25–100. But deepwater drilling gives an EROEI of 10–25. In other words, for every unit of energy used in the extraction process, the resulting oil will only provide 10–25 units of energy in return.

TAR SANDS AND OIL SHALES

If deepwater drilling seems too tricky, what about extracting oil from tar sands?

The total amount of recoverable oil in the Athabasca tar sands in Alberta is estimated to be around a trillion barrels – enough to supply the whole world at current usage rates for thirty years. Unfortunately, the process for getting oil out of tar sands is very expensive, highly polluting and gives a very poor EROEI – something like 3–5. For this reason, supplies from Athabasca are unlikely to increase significantly above the current levels of a million barrels or so a day – possibly enough to secure North America's energy security, but hardly enough to supply growing worldwide demand. Oil shales are similarly problematic in terms of cost, pollution and poor EROEI.

THE POLITICS OF OIL

The most powerful influence on the supply of oil isn't to do with technical challenges, the price of oil or EROEI considerations. It's politics.

About a third of the world's oil production is controlled by OPEC, the Organization of the Petroleum Exporting Countries. Its 12 members are Algeria, Angola, Ecuador, Iran, Iraq, Kuwait, Libya, Nigeria, Qatar, Saudi Arabia, the United Arab Emirates and Venezuela. OPEC members meet regularly to attempt to control the world price and supply of oil. As they control about a third of the world's oil production, their decisions carry a lot of weight. When OPEC decided to restrict oil supplies to the USA in the light of its support for Israel in the 1974 Yom Kippur War, world prices quadrupled in a matter of days.

First among equals in OPEC is Saudi Arabia, which alone produces just over 10mbpd – one barrel in eight of all the oil consumed in the world every day. Saudi Arabia is a fascinating country. Since its foundation in 1932 it's been ruled first by the founder, Abdul Aziz, and then successively by five of his sons. Its current ruler is 88-year-old King Abdullah. Throughout its short history, the country has been marked by extreme tension between the hardline fundamentalist Muslims, of whom Osama bin Laden, the mastermind behind the 9/11 attacks on the USA, is merely one example, and the relatively moderate, fairly pro-Western, royal family who actually rule the country (I say 'relatively moderate' – this is a country where women are still forbidden to vote, drive or do anything much without the permission of a male relative).

Saudi Arabia was largely immune to the unrest spreading through the Arab world in 2011, mainly because of its oil wealth. In 2011 King Abdullah provided sanctuary to the deposed Tunisian dictator Zine El Abidine Ali while announcing a 15 per cent pay increase to state employees. Saudi Arabia, like most

OPEC countries, relies almost entirely on oil revenues to sustain its economy. And oil wealth is a double-edged sword. When oil prices are high, governments like Saudi Arabia's are forced by their people's growing expectations to create more artificial jobs, more subsidies, more major projects. When oil revenues drop, there aren't enough genuine wealth-creating jobs to sustain the economy. This is sometimes known as 'the resource curse', and sometimes as 'the Dutch disease' – when the Netherlands was able to export natural gas for a brief period in the 1960s, the rest of the Dutch economy faltered badly.

If Matt Simmonds is right and Ghawar starts to decline in 2015, Saudi Arabia will face some serious problems. Whether King Abdullah's successor, whoever that is and whenever it happens, will be able to control the inherent tension in the kingdom remains to be seen.

The other Middle Eastern OPEC producers also have their problems. During 2011 there were popular uprisings against autocratic governments in Libya and Iran, partly as a result of these oil-rich states finding that they could no longer afford to subsidise food and fuel quite so generously for their people. The Libyan uprising resulted in the downfall of Muammar Gaddafi; the Iranian protests were suppressed.

The world's second largest producer, with a little under 10mbpd, is Russia, which isn't a member of OPEC. The politics of Russian oil are complex. Three key groups are involved: Vladimir Putin, who has served as both President and Prime Minister of Russia and who controls most of the political power; the so-called oligarchs, a small group of businessmen who own many of the oil and gas companies in Russia, and international companies like BP and Exxon-Mobil which are involved in joint ventures with Russian companies. All three groups need each other, and all three groups mistrust each other in a way that leads to a highly unstable situation.

To give just one example of how this plays out in practice, in January 2011 BP's boss Bob Dudley shook hands with Russian Prime Minister Vladimir Putin. They agreed a $16 billion deal for a joint venture between BP and Rosneft, Russia's state-controlled oil company, to develop Russia's Arctic oilfields. From a business perspective, the deal made sense: Russia gains access to BP's skills, and BP gains access to some unexplored oilfields.

Rosneft's main assets used to belong to a company called Yukos, owned by businessman called Mikhail Khordorkovsky. Some years ago, Khordorkovsky and Putin fell out: Khordorkovsky is now in jail, and the assets of his firm were acquired at a knockdown price by Rosneft, via a mysterious company registered at the address of a vodka bar in Tver, a small town north of Moscow.

Before he became head of BP, Bob Dudley was head of a Russian joint venture called TNK-BP, and he actually fled from Moscow in 2008 in fear for his life when it was intimated that he'd upset some of his Russian business partners. The Russian partners in TNK-BP were very unhappy that BP was now doing a deal with Rosneft, and during the course of 2011 succeeded in scuppering the deal. This left the field open to BP's rival Exxon-Mobil, which signed its deal to exploit the Russian Arctic oilfields with Vladimir Putin in August 2011. Whether this deal can be sustained remains to be seen, but one thing's for sure: some fairly murky politics will continue to play a part in Russian oil and gas production for some time to come.

In summary, then: more than a quarter of the oil we use every day comes from the Middle East or Russia. Both countries are politically sensitive, and don't always have a very positive relationship with the Western world. Relying on them for a major source of energy is a bit of a gamble, which is why US presidents from Richard Nixon to Barack Obama have claimed that it's time to end the USA's addiction to oil. They just haven't yet managed to do it. The world's supplies of cheap conventional oil are in decline. The oil remaining is either technically hard to get at – deepwater, tar sands, oil shales – or under the control of undemocratic regimes, or both. This alone would ensure that the price of oil was set to rise steeply in the years ahead. But it's worse than that – not only is supply becoming more difficult, but demand is soaring.

SOARING DEMAND

Every day the world uses 88 million barrels of oil, mainly for transport – cars, trucks, ships, planes and trains. Since the first commercial production of oil in the early twentieth century, demand for oil has risen steadily, and there's no reason why it should slacken off any time soon. In fact, there are two good reasons why the demand is likely to increase at an even faster rate.

The first reason is the growth of newly emerging economies, especially China and India. In 2010 the average US citizen got through 24 barrels of oil each year, and the average UK citizen about 10. The average Chinese citizen used 2 barrels a year in 2010, and the average Indian just one. But as their economies grow, those countries too will want to use more oil. If every Chinese person used as much oil as the average British person, the world would need an extra 30 million barrels a day. If they used as much as the average American, we'd have to almost double current world production.

Of course, it'll be a few years yet before Chinese and Indian energy consumption approaches European, let alone North American, standards, but other forces are at play. A second reason for increasing energy demands is the growing world population. Currently at around 7 billion, another 500 million people will be joining us over the next ten years or so. They'll want their share of the energy pie. The world's population is predicted to peak at around 9 billion some time in the 2050s. For the next few decades, there'll be more people wanting more energy.

Declining supplies and increasing demand can mean only one thing – an increase in prices. Historically, oil has traded at around $20 a barrel (in real terms) from the beginning of the twentieth century until 1972. After temporarily peaking at around $100 in the wake of the OPEC embargo, it settled down again to around $30 a barrel from 1986 to 2001. From then on, the price began to go steadily upwards to around $80 a barrel in early 2010. The price is quite volatile – there was a spike of $120 in 2008, and $100 in 2011. Where will it be in a year, five years or ten years?

No one knows, but it would be naive to rule out very substantial price rises. Oil companies like Shell and BP will only invest in projects if they see a reasonable likelihood of a decent return. So when Shell invests in tar sands and BP in Arctic oil – both areas where oil costs more than $100 a barrel to extract – you can be sure that oil prices will continue to rise.

While it's impossible to predict the price of oil in the years to come, one thing's certain: if demand continues to rise, the price can only go up. And demand will continue to rise unless the world can find other ways to generate energy, especially for transport – the world's cars, trucks, boats and planes currently depend almost entirely on oil.

Gas

In terms of supply, natural gas is very similar to oil; in many places, natural gas and oil are found together in the same location. The world's largest conventional reserves are to be found in Russia and the Middle East.

In terms of demand, gas fulfils a very different role. Gas is used in industry, for power generation and domestic heating. A major industrial use is the production of nitrogen-based fertiliser, which can more than double crop yields. That's why more than 40 per cent of the running costs of big commercial farms can be fertiliser costs, and that's one of the reasons the price of food is so closely linked to the price of energy. Other industrial uses include the processing of paper, metals, plastics, glass and food – anything that requires heating stuff up.

Domestic heating accounts for about a quarter of all gas usage. Gas also plays a major part in power generation. Twenty per cent of all the world's electricity is generated by burning gas, and in the UK it's 33 per cent, largely thanks to the privatisation of energy generation and distribution by Margaret Thatcher's government in the 1980s. Cheap gas from the North Sea made it economical for the newly privatised generators to begin closing coal-fired power stations and opening gas-fired ones. The so-called 'dash for gas' resulted in a large shift in power generation: in 1990 gas accounted for 38 per cent of all electricity generated.

As a fossil fuel, gas has a big advantage over oil and gas: It produces considerably less carbon dioxide (CO_2). A gas-fired power station produces 30 per cent less CO_2 than an oil-fired one, and 45 per cent less than a coal-fired facility. If governments wanted a relatively quick and economic way to reduce their CO_2 emissions, it would be to replace coal-fired power stations with gas-fired ones.

Unfortunately, you still need the gas to burn, and for many countries, supply is a problem. This is particularly acute in the UK, which has become accustomed to cheap gas from the North Sea. The UK ceased to be self-sufficient in gas in 2006. By 2010, 50 per cent was imported, and this is set to rise to 80 per cent by 2020. At the moment imports are primarily from Norway, but as the Norwegian gas fields will have peaked by 2020, we can expect to become increasingly dependent on the Middle East and Russia. Whether Russia will be keen to sell us gas, and at what price, remains to be seen. In a September 2010 visit to China, Russian President Medvedev said that Russia wanted to supply China with all of its natural gas needs. Meanwhile, back in the UK, there's capacity to store just three weeks' worth of supplies. In January 2010, during a particularly cold winter, the country had just eight days of buffer stocks. Any country which exports gas to Britain would find it easy to use this fuel dependency as a political weapon.

SHALE GAS

What about unconventional supplies of gas? In Canada and some parts of the USA, it's possible to recover large quantities of natural gas held within gas shale, using a process called hydraulic fracturing, or fracking. A conventional gas well is like a conventional oil well – you drill into it and the gas comes pouring out. With shale gas, simply drilling a hole isn't enough: you have to pump in a mixture of water, chemicals and sand at a high enough pressure to fracture the rock and allow the gas to escape. The good news is that there's potentially a lot of shale gas in the ground, especially in North America and China, but also in some European countries. In 2000, shale gas accounted for just 1 per cent of all natural gas supply; by 2011, it was 25 per cent.

The bad news is that it's more expensive to produce than conventional gas, and in some cases there are undesirable side effects. The fracking process can pollute groundwater. According to a recent report from Cornell University, methane released as part of the fracking process may be a significant contributor to global warming. According to the British Geological Survey, it may also cause earthquakes. Work at an experimental shale gas well near Blackpool in Lancashire was suspended in May 2011 after the second of two small earth tremors occurred near the drill site.

Despite these problems, Shale Gas seems to set to transform energy markets, at least in the USA. In 2012 shale gas provides a third of that country's gas supplies, with most predictions suggesting that it could account for half by 2035. The situation in Europe is more complex. Geologically speaking, there are huge quantities of shale gas in Britain, France, Germany and Romania. But in most European countries, mineral rights belong to the state, not to the land owner as in the USA. For this reason European land owners are much less likely to be enthusiastic about drilling for shale gas, especially as the risks are perceived to be more severe in more densely populated countries. New technology may change that of course, but it seems less likely that shale gas will displace other fossil fuels in Europe as it has done in the USA.

Coal

The other big hitter on the fossil fuel stage is coal. Although coal has been used for centuries for heating, it was its use as a fuel for steam engines which kickstarted the Industrial Revolution in the late eighteenth century. Although we don't use steam engines much for transport these days – oil is not only more energy-intense, but being a liquid, it's easier to move around – coal is still an important fuel when it comes to electricity generation. Each day the world burns about 20 million tonnes of the stuff, and most of this is used to drive the turbines in power stations.

Around 40 per cent of the UK's electricity is generated by coal-fired power stations, and the proportion is about the same in the USA. In China, the figure is around 75 per cent.

The good news is that there's plenty left. Worldwide, there's enough coal in the ground to burn it at the current rate for hundreds of years. The USA, for example, which produces all the coal it needs to fuel its coal-fired power stations, has almost 250 years' worth of reserves at current production rates.

The bad news is that coal-fired power is inefficient, polluting and produces lots of CO_2 – a major contributor to global warming.

No form of electricity generation is 100 per cent efficient – even at a hydroelectric power plant, probably the most efficient of conventional energy generation technologies, only 80 per cent of the energy from the flowing water ends up as electricity. But coal-fired plants are the worst. At best, only about 40 per cent of the energy from burning coal ends up as electricity. Most of the rest is lost in heat. That's why you see big cooling towers next to most coal-fired power stations. The coal is pulverised and burnt at high temperatures to convert water into steam; the steam turns turbines to power generators, and is then released into these giant concrete structures which in turn release the heat back into the atmosphere. Forty per cent is actually quite a good figure – some of China's older power stations are only 25 per cent efficient.

The second objection to coal is that burning it is hazardous to human health. Traditional coal-fired power stations emit particulates – very small pieces of coal ash – that can lead to asthma, chronic bronchitis, and an increase in respiratory and cardiac mortality. They also produce various other nasties, including nitrogen oxide and sulphur dioxides, also implicated in negative health effects. That's why the European Union has passed legislation requiring all power generators either to retrofit their power stations with various devices to clean up their act, or to close down altogether. The original legislation, passed in 2001, would have required the closure of a number of coal-fired power stations by 2015 with nothing much to replace them. After lobbying by the UK government, this legislation was amended in 2010 to be tougher in the long term, but give power generators a bit longer to comply – effectively, they now have until 2020, time enough to get some alternatives on stream.

The third objection to coal is the biggest of them all. It's simply that burning coal produces enormous quantities of CO_2, a greenhouse gas. In fact, coal-fired power stations are the single largest source of CO_2 emissions on the planet. In Chapter 2 we'll see why this is such a big issue.

2

Climate Change

*We will face a string of terrible catastrophes unless we act to prepare
ourselves and deal with the underlying causes of global warming.*
                    Al Gore, former Vice President of the United States

*With all of the hysteria, all of the fear, all of the phony science, could it
be that man-made global warming is the greatest hoax ever perpetrated
on the American people? It sure sounds like it.*
                                        US Senator James Inhofe

Who's right? And why should you care?

It's quite hard to get a good, unbiased, overall picture of climate change.
On the one hand there's a significant group of scientists and environmentalists
who think we're doomed. From their perspective, greenhouse gases in the
atmosphere will cause the Earth's average temperature to rise by 6°C or
more, turning most of the world into desert and destroying much of life
on Earth. On the other hand there are the climate sceptics, who say that the
world has been both hotter and cooler in the past, and any climate changes
we're experiencing now are nothing much to worry about. As if this weren't
confusing enough, there are also plenty of well-respected scientists and
environmentalists who claim that climate change is real, but can be dealt with
by a combination of nuclear power, geo-engineering and other technological
solutions that we haven't yet thought of. So what's a level-headed business
leader to believe?

In this chapter I'll outline the science of climate change. I'll explain the basic
facts that are agreed by just about everybody before moving onto the areas that
are more controversial. To begin with, here are three facts that pretty much
everyone agrees on.

The Science of Climate Change

Fact number one: CO_2 is a greenhouse gas. Air that has even a small amount of CO_2 in it will retain more heat than air that doesn't contain CO_2. This is basic science, as basic as the law of gravity. If you hold a stone over the Earth's surface and let go, it will fall to the ground. If you put CO_2 into a jar of air, it will retain heat more than the same jar of air without the CO_2. This is just as well – without current levels of CO_2 in the air, the average global temperature would be 30°C cooler and life might never have evolved on Earth in the first place.

CO_2 is not the only, or the most potent, greenhouse gas. Methane – as emitted, for example, from the farts and belches of cows – is at least 25 times as strong a greenhouse gas as CO_2, and nitrous oxide (N_2O) is pretty potent too. The most widespread greenhouse gas of all is water vapour.

Fact number two: levels of CO_2 in the Earth's atmosphere are rising. Systematic measurement of CO_2 levels in the Earth's atmosphere were first made in 1958 by a scientist called Charles David Keeling. He noticed that CO_2 levels in the atmosphere were rising by about 2 parts per million (ppm) each year. This steady rise has continued pretty much ever since. In 1959 the level was 316ppm; in 2010 the level was 389ppm.

The fact that levels of CO_2 are rising is not controversial. Burning fossil fuels puts carbon dioxide into the atmosphere. Burning a gallon of petrol in a typical car's engine produces about 8 kilograms of CO_2; burning a cubic metre of gas in your central heating boiler produces about 2 kilograms, and burning a tonne of coal in a traditional pulverised coal-fired power station produces upwards of 2,000 kilograms. Every day on this planet we burn 88 million barrels of oil, 10 billion cubic metres of gas and 20 million tonnes of coal, so it really shouldn't surprise us that we put 86 million tonnes of CO_2 into the atmosphere every day, or about 1,000 tonnes a second.

What happens to it? Quite a lot of it is absorbed by plants and trees, which effectively breathe in carbon dioxide and expel oxygen as a waste product. Quite a lot of it is absorbed in the oceans, mainly by algae that absorb it, die and fall to the seabed. But less is absorbed than is produced, so the levels keep rising.

Fact number three: the Earth is getting warmer. The average increase in global temperature is generally accepted to be 0.74°C since pre-industrial times – generally taken to be 1800. It's quite tricky to arrive at this figure. The Earth's temperature can vary from more than 40°C in the tropics to less than minus 40°C at the pole. The temperature at a given location can vary by 5°C in a day, and 60°C over the course of a year. Cities tend to be warmer than the surrounding countryside because they absorb, generate and retain more heat than rural areas. Accurate temperature measuring equipment has only been around for the past few decades. If you want to monitor temperatures back to the start of the nineteenth century, you're relying on ships' captains with dodgy thermometers, and secondary data like the size of tree rings. Despite this complexity, by analysing a lot of data with some nifty computers, scientists are pretty much agreed that the Earth has warmed by 0.74°C since 1800.

If you look at the warming of the Earth's land mass, rather than the entire planet, including the oceans, the change is even more dramatic. According to independent studies by NASA and the National Oceanic and Atmospheric Administration (NOAA) in the USA, and a joint study by Britain's Meteorological Office and the University of East Anglia's Climate Research Unit, the land has warmed by 0.9°C in just the last fifty years. According to the Met Office, most of the UK has experienced a 1°C rise in temperature in the thirty years between 1980 and 2010.

Three indisputable facts: CO_2 is a greenhouse gas, CO_2 levels are rising, and the world is getting warmer. But has this small rise in global temperature actually been caused by increasing quantities of CO_2 that we're putting into the air? Maybe it's all just a big coincidence. Perhaps the rise in global temperatures is due to natural variation, and has little or nothing to do with human beings burning fossil fuels. After all, the Earth was 7°C warmer 55 million years ago, and that couldn't be blamed on people because there weren't any.

Over very long timescales the Earth's temperature has indeed changed significantly, with volcanic eruptions, tectonic plate shifts and even crashing meteorites all being implicated. What's different this time is the speed of the change. As far as the boffins can tell, prehistoric changes in global temperature have taken thousands of years; the recent change of almost 1°C in just a few hundred years is unprecedented. Despite attempts by a very small group of people to attribute this to changes on the surface of the Sun, or some other as yet unknown natural process, pretty much every scientist who's studied the subject agrees that the recent rise in global temperatures is most likely to have been caused by human beings putting CO_2 and other greenhouse gases into the air.

Here's the view from the US National Academy of Sciences:

> *Climate change is occurring, is caused largely by human activities …*
> *and in many cases is already affecting a broad range of human and*
> *natural systems.*

Here's the UK's Royal Society:

> *There is strong evidence that the warming of the Earth over the last*
> *half-century has been caused largely by human activity, such as the*
> *burning of fossil fuels and changes in land use, including agriculture*
> *and deforestation.*

And even Nigel Lawson, a leading British climate change sceptic, says:

> *Given the greenhouse effect, it can also be said to be settled science*
> *that the marked, and largely man-made, increase in carbon dioxide*
> *concentrations in the atmosphere has contributed to the modest*
> *twentieth-century warming of the planet.*

Although the burning of fossil fuels is the major culprit in increasing atmospheric levels of CO_2 and other greenhouse gases, it's not the only one. As the Royal Society noted in the quotation above, agriculture and deforestation play a significant role also. Around 18 per cent of all greenhouse gas emissions caused by human beings are related to agriculture: Most of the world's commercial farming relies on nitrogen-based fertilisers, which release nitrous oxide, a potent greenhouse gas. Methane is produced from rice cultivation and in the belches and farts of cows and other livestock. Deforestation releases CO_2 directly into the atmosphere as wood is burnt or rots, and prevents the natural absorption of CO_2 that would have occurred if the forest had remained.

The Effects of Global Warming

So far so good: human beings have put a lot of CO_2 and other greenhouse gases into the atmosphere over the last two hundred years, and that seems to have contributed to a very modest warming – less than 1°C – in the average global temperature. Why should we care? Surely such a small rise in temperature can't matter much? It might even be a good thing – don't crops and people like a bit of warmth?

While it's true that the effects of a 0.74°C rise in temperatures have been fairly minimal to date, the Earth will continue to warm. Even if all CO_2 emissions ceased today, the accumulated CO_2 (and other greenhouse gases) in the atmosphere would cause the Earth to continue warming for decades. And far from ceasing greenhouse gas emissions, we are currently increasing them. The effects of temperature rises of 2°C or more are both significant and overwhelmingly negative. They fall into two main categories – changing weather patterns and a rise in sea levels.

CHANGING WEATHER PATTERNS

Here's how the world's weather works. Hot, damp air rises over the equator, and moves towards the poles. Once it gets to the temperate zones, it cools and the water vapour condenses as rain. The somewhat drier air flows back towards the equator, warming and absorbing water vapour as it goes, and the cycle begins once again. The overall picture is that land close to the equator tends to be hot and humid (think Amazon rainforest), land a bit further away from the equator tends to be hot and dry (think Sahara desert), and places further away from the equator than that tend to be warm with reasonable rainfall (think Britain or the Midwest of America).

The rotation of the Earth skews things round a bit, which is why the trade winds tend to go diagonally rather than purely north or south as you'd expect from my simple explanation, and the irregular shape of the continents ruffles this basic pattern into one of almost unimaginable complexity. Ocean currents, seasonal variations and regional effects like the Arctic oscillation, which gave Britons cold winters in 2009 and 2010, and the El Niño/La Niña oscillation which flooded Australia, Brazil and Sri Lanka in 2011 all add to the complexity, but the basic pattern remains.

Global warming subtly alters this pattern. As the Earth becomes warmer, the hot, wet air which rises over the equator stays warmer longer as it makes its journey towards the poles. Instead of cooling and raining where it does now, it will travel a bit further towards the poles before the water vapour condenses as rain. What this means is that the temperate zones, which happen to be the major food-producing areas of the world, will become warmer and drier than they are now.

This will have a big impact on food production. Most staple crops – wheat, rice, maize – are surprisingly sensitive to changes in temperature and humidity.

An average rise of just 1°C, for example, will reduce the yield of a rice field by 30 per cent.

In the developed countries of the world, less agriculture means less food available to export; in developing countries it is a recipe for mass starvation. Actually, it's worse than that: reduced rainfall also means reduced water supplies, and global warming will exacerbate the situation of over a billion people who already live in areas where water is short. Changing patterns of rainfall and temperature also have a big impact on wildlife. Some species will adapt or migrate, others will become extinct.

How severe will these changes be, and how quickly will they happen? This is where the climate science becomes more controversial. Some say that we could see dramatic changes in just a few years. Others say that we have decades, even centuries, to adjust to change. No one knows for sure. The world's system for producing and distributing food is very delicately balanced – it doesn't take much to throw the system out of kilter. In 2011 poor Russian harvests and floods in Australia drove the price of wheat to record levels. This in turn contributed to rising food prices across the world, and this in turn led to political unrest in many countries, including Tunisia and Egypt, where the government was driven from power. This is not the first, nor will it be the last, government to fall ultimately as a result of the weather. We'll explore this further in Chapter 8, which is all about the possible conflicts that may arise as a result of climate change.

To what extent are we already seeing changing weather patterns as a result of climate change? Were those poor Russian harvests and Australian floods, along with Hurricane Katrina and the hot European summer of 2003, caused by climate change, or just the kind of natural variation in the weather you'd expect?

This is a surprisingly tricky question to answer, and is usually sidestepped with the response that climate change makes extreme weather events more likely. The truth is a little more nuanced. Munich Re is one of the world's largest reinsurance firms. When a traditional insurance company faces huge payouts as a result of some natural disaster, it avoids going bust because it has insured itself against that risk with a reinsurer like Munich Re. In order to charge its customers the right premiums, Munich Re needs to have a pretty good idea about how often natural disasters will occur and how much damage they will cause. It's not interested in debates about climate science – it just wants to know what effect a changing climate will have. So what does Munich Re think about climate change and extreme weather events? According to its research, flood-related disasters have tripled in the last thirty years, and wind-related disasters have doubled. In comparison, non-weather-related disasters – earthquakes and volcanoes – have remained pretty constant. Even taking into account the fact that there are more people on the planet, and they are choosing to live in places vulnerable to natural disasters – flood plains and coastal areas generally – Munich Re concludes that the only plausible conclusion is that these extreme weather events are climate-related.

RISING SEA LEVELS

The second major effect of climate change is a rise in sea levels. Currently, sea levels are rising by an average of 2 millimetres each year. Water expands as it gets warmer, and this modest rise in sea levels is caused by the gradual warming of the last two hundred years or so. This gradual rise is nothing much to worry about. Unfortunately, this rate is set to rise dramatically, and here's why.

An awful lot of the world's ice floats on the surface of the sea. Most of the Arctic falls into this category, which is why it's possible to sail underneath it in a submarine. If global warming causes it all to melt, overall sea levels won't change, for the same reason that the level of liquid in your gin and tonic doesn't change when the ice cube floating in your glass melts. But ice that's sitting on land is a different matter. When it melts, the sea level does rise. The Greenland ice shelf covers an area the size of France and is on average a mile thick. If this all melted, sea levels would rise by about 7 metres. What are the chances of this happening?

Unfortunately, very high. In fact, it's already melting, but at a reasonably slow rate. When the average global temperature has risen by 2°C, this rate of melting will increase dramatically, with some scientists suggesting that it could all be gone within a hundred years. The resulting 7 metre rise in sea levels would inundate London, New York, Hong Kong, Mumbai and all the other major world cities that are built on low-lying land near the coast.

Of course it's not just the Greenland ice shelf that would go in a warmer world, it's most of the other land-based ice as well. The last time the world was pretty much ice-free was in the Pliocene period, three million years ago. The world was an average 3°C warmer, and sea levels were 25 metres higher than today.

The 2°C Tipping Point

Climate change, in common with many other kinds of change in business, politics and individuals, doesn't happen gradually and smoothly; it happens in fits and starts. For a long time, it appears that very little is changing, until we reach a tipping point, when change happens very quickly indeed. Many scientists believe that there will be a tipping point at around 2°C, and the evidence is convincing enough for many politicians to see 2°C as a tipping point too. At this temperature, not only will the rate of ice sheet melting dramatically increase, but something else very significant will happen too: the melting of permanently frozen ground in Russia – the Siberian permafrost.

Actually, it's melting a little bit already, which is why you can find pictures on the Internet of wonky Russian houses and factories where the foundations have collapsed as the permafrost turned to mush, but at 2°C the rate of melting really speeds up. The Siberian permafrost contains a lot of methane; as it melts, that methane is released into the atmosphere; methane is a very potent greenhouse gas which leads to further global warming. So although it's taken us two hundred years to register less than 1°C of global warming, with all this extra methane doing its bit, the next rise of 1°C could take just a few decades.

Although the world has warmed by 0.74°C since pre-industrial times, the rise hasn't been steady throughout that period. The world actually cooled a little between 1860 and 1910, and again from 1940 to 1950; but the overall trend is upwards, with a rise of 0.2°C a decade for the past twenty years. If this is sustained, we'll have an overall rise of 2°C somewhere around 2080. But we won't maintain CO_2 at 2010 levels. CO_2 levels are continuing to rise by 2 ppm each year, and may rise even faster than that. If countries continue to increase their CO_2 emissions at current rates, we could hit the critical 2°C by as early as 2040.

Climate change is already happening. It's caused by human beings putting greenhouse gases into the atmosphere. If global warming continues, it will lead to bad consequences. This we know for sure. What we don't know with any degree of precision is how quickly the world will continue to warm up, how soon those bad things will happen, and how devastating they will be when they do.

Three Strategies for Action

Given that the world will continue to get warmer, but that we can't be sure how fast or with what consequences, what action should we take? There are three broad strategies to choose from. Which strategy – or combination of strategies – you opt for depends largely on how soon and how severely you think the bad consequences will kick in.

Strategy number one is mitigation: try to stop further global warming by limiting our emissions of greenhouse gases. Most governments have publicly adopted climate change mitigation as one of their key policy goals. The UK, for example, is committed to reducing CO_2 emissions by 34 per cent by 2020 and 80 per cent by 2050, and many countries have adopted similar targets. Although these targets are noble aspirations, they're very unlikely to be achieved, and even if they did, wouldn't halt global warming. The amount of CO_2 in the atmosphere today is already sufficient to enable the climate to continue to warm for decades to come. Nevertheless, the fact that governments have adopted them and are putting in place various mechanisms to try and achieve them creates threats and opportunities for business, which we will explore later.

Strategy number two is adaptation: accept that the world will get warmer and bad consequences will happen, then try to adapt to this. Rising sea levels and extreme weather? Build higher sea walls or move the cities. Not enough rainfall to grow current crops? Better irrigation or new, less thirsty, breeds of plant. The problem with adaptation is that we may not be able to adapt quickly enough if the consequences turn out to be rather severe. Nevertheless, every business should take adaptation seriously, to ensure that its current business model can continue to function in a changing world, but also because adaptation also creates lots of opportunities for new business.

The biggest fans of adaptation used to be the so-called climate change sceptics, those people who believe that climate change is not man-made, but a natural phenomenon caused by the Sun, or the Earth wobbling on it axis, or by some as yet unexplained natural phenomenon that we can't do anything about. The sceptic's argument is that if the Earth will get warmer anyway, whatever we do about fossil fuels, we might as well focus our efforts on adapting to the inevitable changes. In recent years, the climate sceptics have been joined by another group of people who are also enthusiastic about adaptation. This group believes that man-made emissions are responsible for global warming, but that it's now too late to prevent significant temperature rise over the next few decades. Most members of this group would continue to advocate mitigation measures – reducing CO_2 emissions by moving towards a low-carbon economy – but accept that whatever we do now isn't going to be enough.

Mitigation and adaptation may be all we need. Or it may not. In which case, we can turn to strategy number three, the strategy that dare not speak its name, the strategy that until recently was all but taboo even to speak about: geo-engineering. Geo-engineering means cooling the world, not by reducing the amount of greenhouse gases we put into the atmosphere, but more directly – by blocking out some of the sunlight hitting the planet, or by sucking out of the atmosphere some of the CO_2 that's already there.

Geo-engineering is a relative newcomer to the climate change debate, and a highly controversial one. Instead of reducing greenhouse gas emissions or trying to adapt to a hotter world, why not take more direct approaches to cooling the planet? You could block off some of the Sun's rays, either by putting mirrors in space (a totally unfeasible, mad idea) or by spraying particles of dust into the atmosphere (quite plausible) or by making clouds whiter so they reflect more sunlight into space (feasible and cheap). Alternatively, you could invent some gizmo to suck all the CO_2 out of the air and either bury it or turn it into aviation fuel (probably quite a long way off). Geo-engineering currently has few fans, and vigorous opponents, but that could change if a decade or two's attempts at mitigation and adaptation turn out to fail. There are business opportunities too in geo-engineering, but probably only for a small number of very innovative companies.

Responding to climate change creates both opportunities and threats for business. In the next chapter we'll examine how governments, businesses and individuals are responding to climate change.

3

Responding to the Challenge of Climate Change

Business is the force of change. Business is essential to solving the climate crisis, because this is what business is best at: innovating, changing, addressing risks, searching for opportunities. There is no more vital task.

Richard Branson, entrepreneur

Your success as a business ultimately depends on whether individual consumers choose to buy your products or not. This is true whether you supply directly to consumers (B2C), or whether you supply to other businesses (B2B) – it's just that the ultimate purchaser is further away down your customer chain. In the first part of this chapter we'll look at the ways individual consumer behaviour is and isn't changing as a result of climate change.

However, no business is entirely free to deal with customers however it wishes. Every business operates in a legal and regulatory framework that is determined by government. Many national and local governments are taking climate change very seriously and acting in a way that creates both opportunities and threats for business.

Finally in this chapter we'll take a look at the role that businesses themselves are taking to drive us towards the low-carbon economy.

Individuals

How seriously are people concerned about climate change? According to a report commissioned by the World Bank in 2009, a majority of respondents in 14 out of the 15 countries surveyed not only believed that climate change was a major concern, but they expressed a willingness to commit resources to combat climate change. In China, 67 per cent said that there should be limitations on coal-fired power plants, even if this increases the cost of energy. Even in the USA 63 per cent were willing to spend at least 0.5 per cent of GDP on combating climate change. Only in Russia did less than half of the respondents wish to take action against climate change.

Although the UK was not included in this international survey, polls at the time reflect a similar picture. A 2009 *Guardian*/ICM survey found that three out of four Britons considered climate change to be an important problem.

If most people feel so strongly about global warming, why is there so little obvious change in people's behaviour?

There are three reasons. One of the many quirks of being human is that we respond well to short-term threats and badly to long-term threats. If we're walking down a dark alley at night and hear a strange sound, our heart immediately starts pumping harder to get us ready to run away from whatever immediate danger may lurk in the shadows. But if our financial adviser says we need to be saving more for our retirement, some years into the future, our eyes glaze over and we prefer to think about something else. That's why more than half of the UK's pensioners have an income of less than £10,000 and 8 million UK workers have no pension provision at all. Climate change feels like an ill-defined threat that is a long way in the future, and this means, for most individuals, that there is no incentive for taking action.

The second reason why most people don't take action on climate change or energy security is their entirely reasonable belief that individual actions won't make a difference, given what everyone else is doing. If I give up driving and take the bus, everyone else will continue to drive. If I decide to stop flying, the plane will fly anyway. This logic can be scaled up to national levels. If all 60 million of us in the UK reduce our energy consumption, that will be wiped out by the increasing energy usage of 1.3 billion Chinese.

These reasons would be enough in themselves to prevent people changing, but the third reason is the most compelling of all: most people won't change if it involves more cost or less convenience. We could reduce out CO_2 emissions by a third and our consumption of oil in the UK by 80 per cent if we wanted to, simply by switching over to electric cars: but we haven't yet, because in 2012 electric cars are more expensive and less convenient.

It's this third factor that trumps the other two. The best way to get people to change their behaviour is to make it cheaper and more convenient to do so. If electric cars were cheaper to buy, cheaper to run and more convenient than internal combustion engine cars, then almost everyone would buy them. What's true for cars is true for everything else in the low-carbon economy. That's why governments play a key role in creating a context in which low-carbon products and services can become cheaper and better than their fossil fuel equivalents.

There are some exceptions to the rule that money and convenience trumps everything else. There is a small group of people who are willing to pay more, because of their values and beliefs about the environment. These people will pay more for renewable energy, green buildings, organic food, socially responsible investments and so on. The marketers sometimes refer to this market segment as LOHAS – Lifestyles Of Health And Sustainability – and according to some figures as many as 16 per cent of consumers fit into this category.

I began this section by referring to some attitude surveys to climate change which were conducted in 2009 – just before an important and well-publicised climate summit which took place in Copenhagen in December of that year. How have opinions changed since? As I write this in 2012, the general trend hasn't changed much – in 2011, for example, a Rasmussen poll found that 58 per cent of Americans see climate change as a serious problem, and 33 per cent see it as a very serious problem.

Governments

> *Now look, I'm a free market capitalist. You have to be, to be running GE. There is no mistake. That is the framework I come from. I grew up in. I have been trained to be suspicious of every government in all activities just like they are suspicious of us in all activities. But the energy challenge won't be met unless the governments play an active, directive and responsible role.*
>
> *Jeff Immelt, Chairman, GE*

Governments can influence the low-carbon agenda in many ways. Many governments have set legally binding targets for greenhouse gas emissions, as well as employing a variety of carrots and sticks to try to encourage individuals and organisations to reduce their greenhouse gas emissions and become more energy-efficient. In this section we'll take a close look at what the UK government is doing, which is fairly typical of many European governments. We'll then consider the very different approaches taken by the USA and China.

In 2008 the then Labour government set a target to reduce UK greenhouse gas emissions by 34 per cent by 2020 and 80 per cent by 2050 (against a 1990 baseline). In 2010 the incoming Conservative/Liberal Democrat coalition government not only confirmed its commitment to this target, but claimed it wanted to be 'the greenest government ever'.

MORE RENEWABLE ENERGY

If the UK is to reduce its carbon emissions by 34 per cent by 2020, there will need to be a huge increase in energy from renewable sources and nuclear. While nuclear will almost certainly form an important part of the energy mix for most countries – in 2009 the Labour government gave the green light for ten new nuclear power stations in the UK – nuclear energy is still controversial, both in terms of safety and cost. For this reason most governments are focusing on the development of renewable energy.

In 2012 only 7 per cent of all electricity generated in the UK comes from renewable sources. Roughly half of this is hydroelectric power, and half wind. In order to stimulate more renewable energy, UK governments have taken two approaches: the Renewables Obligation and Feed-in Tariffs (FITs).

The Renewables Obligation scheme began in 2002. Each year the government sets a target for the proportion of energy each supplier must generate from renewable sources. In 2002 it was 3 per cent. By 2010 it was 11.1 per cent in England and Wales (the figures are different for Scotland and Northern Ireland), and it will rise to 15.4 per cent by 2015. Suppliers are granted Renewable Obligation Certificates (ROCs) for each megawatt hour (MWh) they generate from renewables, and these can be sold on the open market to other suppliers who fail to meet their obligation. In effect, it is a financial incentive for power companies to generate more renewable energy. In some ways the scheme has been a success: the amount of renewable power has more than doubled since 2002, largely thanks to a few large windfarms. However, the scheme has done little to promote more risky renewable technologies such as solar, wave and tidal energy.

That's where FITs come in. Largely aimed at households and small businesses, the scheme guarantees a fixed payment over a long period (often

25 years) for small-scale generators. If you chose to put a small solar panel on the roof of your house in 2011, the government would have paid you an index-related 41.3p for every kilowatt hour (kWh) of electricity you generated, even if you used the power yourself. If you didn't use it, but exported it back to the grid, you got paid another 3p per kWh. The exact numbers depend on the type and size of the power source, and when and how it was installed.

Feed-in tariffs have been in operation for some time in many other European countries, most notably in Germany. Thanks to FITs, Germany now has almost 2 billion watts (2GW) of solar power generation (equivalent to two coal-fired power stations) and is key player in solar photovoltaic technology. Solar power is still more expensive than electricity from coal-fired power stations, but could reach grid parity – be as cheap as fossil fuel power – by as early as 2014.

As I write this in 2012 the government is still reviewing its energy policy with a view to generating a third of the UK's electricity from renewable sources by 2020, while maintaining energy security at a reasonable price for consumers. Proposed measures include strengthening Feed-in Tariffs to give suppliers more long-term certainty, a moratorium on new coal-fired power stations unless they are equipped to capture and store the CO_2 emissions, better provision for standby power to cope with peak demands, and a floor on the price of carbon.

The UK has also signed up to the EU's Renewable Energy Directive, which requires the UK to develop 15 per cent of all its energy from renewable sources by 2020. In order to achieve this, 30 per cent of electricity generation, 12 per cent of heating and 10 per cent of transport would need to be powered from renewable sources.

In recent years UK governments have generally done a reasonable job of encouraging power generating companies to do more with renewables. The amount of power from renewable sources in the UK has doubled over the last five years, admittedly from a very low base. Most of this has been wind power – a relatively cheap and uncontroversial form of non-fossil fuel. The challenge over the next few years will be to encourage other forms of renewables, not least because we are fast running out of space for windfarms.

The fact remains that in 2012 renewable energy is still more expensive than fossil fuel energy and requires some kind of government subsidy to encourage the innovation and economies of scale that will help to bring prices down, and feed-in tariffs have been extremely successful at doing that. In November 2011, however, the UK government announced that it intended to halve the rate paid for small-scale solar photovoltaic energy from 43.3p per kWh to just 21p. This is bad news for the developing renewable energy sector in the UK, but the decision has wider consequences: businesses want a stable regulatory and fiscal framework in which to develop, not one that changes unpredictably and inconsistently. It also starkly contradicts UK Prime Minister David Cameron's claim of May 2010 to be the 'greenest government ever'.

BETTER ENERGY EFFICIENCY

The second way in which governments can respond to the threats of climate change and energy security is to encourage people and businesses to be more energy-efficient. One stick with which governments like to beat their people is taxation, and in the UK there are at least three forms of carbon tax – the Climate Change Levy, the CRC (Carbon Reduction Commitment) scheme and the EU emissions trading scheme.

The Climate Change Levy is a tax on electricity and gas which applies to all consumers. It is set at too low a level to have any significant effect on consumption. Despite an increase to more than 5 million of the number of people in the UK living in fuel poverty (defined as spending more than 10 per cent of income on domestic energy costs), the Climate Change Levy has not encouraged people to be more frugal with their energy.

The CRC energy efficiency scheme is aimed at large organisations – those who spend more than around £500,000 on electricity each year. The details are quite complex, and vary slightly from year to year, but the basic principle is this: participating companies must purchase a permit to cover every tonne of CO_2 they emit. In the first few years of the scheme permits cost £12 per tonne, so a company with an annual electricity bill of £500,000 would need about £40,000 worth of permits.

In the original formulation of the scheme, which was devised by the Labour government in 2009, the money raised from the sale of permits was to have been given back to the companies that had made the biggest reductions in CO_2 emissions over the previous year, but in Conservative Chancellor George Osborne's autumn 2010 spending review it was announced that this money will now by retained by government.

The CRC scheme has had a big impact on the businesses affected, and the combined effect of the CRC with generally rising energy costs has driven many businesses to become much more energy-efficient.

As well as implementing its home-grown legislation, the UK is also subject to legislation from the European Community. The EU Emissions Trading Scheme (ETS) was designed to reduce the CO_2 emissions of some of Europe's most energy-intensive industries, like power generation, steel production and cement manufacture. Unlike the Climate Change Levy, which is a simple tax, the ETS is a cap and trade scheme. This means that an overall limit is set on carbon emissions (the cap), and companies buy permits to allow emissions up to that level. They can buy or sell these permits (the trade bit).

If a company uses more than a certain amount of energy, it must buy permits for each tonne of CO_2 produced – the so called carbon price. As this is a cap and trade scheme, companies who wish to buy or sell permits can do so, and there is a thriving market in ETS permits – except when the market was temporarily suspended in January 2011 after cybercriminals stole €7 million worth of permits from the Czech carbon register.

The ETS scheme has not been a great success. Although greenhouse emissions across the EU have declined, this has been more to do with the recession than with the ETS. Because of the way member countries were allowed to allocate permits in the first place, too many permits were doled out, which means that the price at which they are traded remains low – so much so that some companies were hoarding permits in case they need them for further use. Cap and trade schemes tend to be very bureaucratic, and divert resources into trading and administration activities.

Finally, although the steel and cement industries do produce a lot of CO_2, it doesn't make a lot of sense to penalise these industries in Europe when they are facing a lot of competition, especially in China and India, and when we need a lot of steel and cement to build a low-carbon energy generation and transmission infrastructure. It takes a lot of steel and cement to build a windfarm, let alone a nuclear power station.

Perhaps the most significant piece of UK legislation on climate change is due to be enacted in 2012 and this is concerned with carbon disclosure. At present about half of the FTSE 350 companies measure and report publicly on their carbon footprint – less than 10 per cent of all companies currently do so. The 2008 Climate Change Act that set the 2020 and 2050 targets also mandated the government to introduce compulsory reporting on greenhouse gas emissions by 12 April 2012, or explain to Parliament why it has not done so. Shortly before the 12 April deadline the current UK coalition government announced that it would not be introducing compulsory greenhouse gas emission monitoring for some unspecified time. The deferral of this decision was heavily criticised by business, and described as a real source of frustration by the Confederation of British Industry.

LOW-CARBON TRANSPORT

Given that 25 per cent of all CO_2 emissions in the UK are caused by transport, you could reduce emissions either by discouraging driving or by persuading people to drive more efficient cars.

UK fuel prices are amongst the highest in the world, thanks to a very high rate of tax. In 2011 petrol cost around £1.30 a litre, of which 66 per cent was tax – a mixture of VAT and fuel tax. Taxing the cost of fuel is problematic for two reasons. First, it is politically very unpopular. Protests by motorists caused the then Labour government to abandon its plans to continue raising fuel taxes in 2003. In early 2011, when pump prices rose sharply, partly as a result of higher oil prices and partly as a result of the increase in VAT from 17.5 per cent to 20 per cent, there were once again mutterings from motorists and talk from the government about introducing some kind of fuel price stabiliser, effectively reducing fuel tax if the price of oil increased. Meddling with the cost of motoring is politically very tricky.

Perhaps the biggest disadvantage of taxing the cost of fuel is that it doesn't appear to do very much to deter motorists from driving. In 2001, when motorists were protesting at fuel costing 65p a litre, the average UK motorist clocked up around 7,000 miles each year. In 2011, with the price at the pump around 130p a litre, the average driver clocked up more that 9,500 miles a year – an increase of some 35 per cent.

A better approach is to encourage people to drive more efficient cars. Since 2001 Vehicle Excise Duty, more commonly known as road tax, has been determined by the vehicle's CO_2 emissions. Any vehicle emitting less than 100g/km pays nothing, while a car that produces more than 225g/km pays £435. This appears to have been modestly successful: the average CO_2 emissions of new cars sold in the UK has dropped by about 10 per cent in the ten years since the scheme was introduced.

Overall, though, the government has been unsuccessful in reducing the energy use and CO_2 emissions of transport. The most effective way to do this would simply be to allow fuel costs to rise even faster than they do now, but this is politically difficult. Most motorists are voters, and the motoring lobby is a very powerful one.

The government also offers to subsidise 25 per cent of the cost of a new electric car (up to a maximum of £5,000) and has invested £20 million in battery recharging points throughout the UK.

OTHER EUROPEAN GOVERNMENTS

Most European governments have taken a broadly similar approach to that in the UK. They've set targets for CO_2 emissions (generally in the range 20–30 per cent for 2020, and around 80 per cent for 2050). Countries like Germany that rely heavily on fossil fuels have used FITs and other incentives to encourage more power generation from renewables, in order to meet the European community target of 20 per cent of electricity generation in each member state coming from renewable sources by 2020. Germany now has more than 5GW of installed solar power and 23GW of installed wind power thanks to generous FITs. Of course, some European countries already generate much of their power from low-carbon sources. France, Sweden and Switzerland already generate more than 90 per cent of their electricity from a mixture of nuclear and hydroelectric power.

Most European countries tax energy usage in order to encourage energy efficiency, including fuel tax on road vehicles. Historically, fuel taxes in Europe have been higher than in the USA, and this is one of the main reasons why the average European citizen has a carbon footprint half the size of the average US citizen.

THE USA

Although the USA was recently overtaken by China to be the world's largest producer of greenhouse gases, it remains the per capita global champion at putting CO_2 into the atmosphere. The USA is also one of the few major industrial countries that has made no commitment to reducing its carbon emissions. After the 2009 Copenhagen conference, which ended in shambles, President Obama committed the USA to a meagre 4 per cent cut in greenhouse gas emissions by 2020 (compared to 1990 levels), but even this modest proposal was thrown out be the US Senate. Why is the USA so exceptionalist when it comes to climate change and energy security? Part of the problem is the USA's highly partisan political system. Broadly speaking, Democratic politicians believe climate change is real and are willing to take action to combat it, whereas Republican politicians believe that climate change, if it's happening at all, is not man-made, and that any action to prevent it will harm jobs. The result is political stalemate. This political impasse is one of the reasons the USA is in decline, according to Tom Friedman and Michael Mandelbaum, whose book *That Used To Be Us* is a wonderful analysis of what went wrong with America. Despite the fact that Americans virtually invented the environmental movement, and that the Environmental Protection Agency, created by Republican Richard Nixon in 1970, was a role model for similar organisations the world over, the USA in the twenty-first century is clearly unable to take a lead on climate change.

What's particularly interesting about the USA is that despite the lack of leadership at national level, some states and many cities are making huge progress in transforming themselves into low-carbon economies. Portland, Oregon is one of the world's greenest cities: half of its power comes from renewable sources and a quarter of the workforce commutes by bike or public transport. Even New York City has an ambitious plan to combat climate change and enhance the quality of life for New Yorkers while strengthening the local economy. This includes a commitment to reduce the city's greenhouse gas emissions by 30 per cent by 2030.

CHINA

If the world's largest democracy struggles to make progress on tackling climate change, how about the world's biggest one-party state? Those who rule this country of 1.3 billion people have a delicate balancing act to maintain. As engineers (President Hu Jintao was a hydroelectric engineer before he got into politics) they know that climate change is real and that it's already having a mainly negative effect on their country. As unelected rulers they know that they can maintain power only as long as the country continues to achieve extraordinary levels of growth. The government's latest five-year plan reflects that need for balance. Growth will continue at 7 per cent (a reduction on the 11 per cent annual growth achieved during the previous five-year plan), but by 2015 non-fossil fuel energy will account for 11.4 per cent of total energy use, and there will be a 17 per cent reduction in carbon-intensity, as measured by greenhouse gas emissions per unit of GDP.

What Chance International Agreements?

During the 1970s scientists were becoming increasingly concerned about part of the Earth's stratosphere popularly known as the ozone layer. The amount of ozone appeared to be in decline, mainly as a result of chlorofluorocarbons (CFCs), a chemical widely used in refrigerators and aerosol spray cans. Since the ozone layer protects the surface of the Earth from harmful ultraviolet radiation, this was considered to be health risk. It was estimated that a 10 per cent loss of ozone above the UK would lead to an extra 8,000 cases of skin cancer each year. Although some businesses (including manufacturers of CFCs) argued that it was far from certain that CFCs were depleting the ozone layer, that the risks to health were much exaggerated, and that restricting use of CFCs would have catastrophic economic effects, in 1979 the USA banned the use of CFCs in spray cans. In 1989 an international agreement was signed in Montreal to limit consumption of CFCs, with 191 countries eventually signing up. The Montreal Protocol is widely seen as a success, with ozone levels increasing to their former levels as the use of CFCs declines to almost nothing.

So if we can do it with CFCs, why can't we do it with greenhouse gases? If the Montreal Protocol was such a success, why was the international climate change conference in Copenhagen in 2009 such an utter failure?

The answer is partly a question of scale, partly a question of alternatives, but mainly a question of history. Although CFC production and use was a major industry in many countries, it was only a fraction of the size of the power generation industry. Technologically, it was very easy to produce alternatives to CFCs; alternatives to fossil fuel power are not so easily available at the cost of fossil fuels. But the failure of the international climate change conference in Copenhagen in 2009 and other attempts to reach international agreements on limiting greenhouse gas emissions essentially boil down to history. Developed countries were willing to make quite substantial cuts providing the developing world agreed to keep emissions very low. But this would effectively deny the developing nations the opportunities for growth that cheap fossil fuel offers. So that kind of a deal was never going to happen. Here's what the developing nations thought:

> *You – the developed world – have spent the last two hundred years chucking greenhouse gases into the atmosphere, and enjoying the fruits of growth. We can see that climate change is happening, but please don't penalise our growth prospects for your previous mistakes. The only deal we'll be happy with is for us to have our fair share of the growth that hydrocarbons deliver, while your economies pretty much stop emitting greenhouse gases altogether. We know that this will harm your economies, but if you think climate change is a serious as you say it is, surely that is a price you would be willing to pay?*

As you can imagine, no leader of a Western democracy would survive very long if he or she had to sell that kind of a deal to his or her electorate. That's why agreement wasn't reached at Copenhagen, and probably never will be at any international summit. The only way to reduce CO_2 emissions is to develop an economy that thrives just as much on non-fossil fuel sources of energy as high-carbon economies do now.

Businesses

How are businesses responding to the challenge of climate change? Like individuals and governments, businesses are responding in different ways.

A few are ignoring the challenge. It's hard to see how they do this, with rising energy costs hitting the bottom line and growing legislation around climate change. However there are some businesses which take the position that climate change probably isn't happening, but if it is, the affects will be so far in the future that they needn't be concerned.

To ignore climate change is to misunderstand the fundamental concept of business risk. Every business needs to think about the bad things that might happen in the future, and what it can do now either to prevent those bad things happening, or to reduce their impact when they do. The chances that your offices or store or factory might catch fire and burn to the ground are quite small; but you still take action to prevent it happening – smoke detectors, sprinkler systems – and to minimise the impact if it does – typically building insurance.

A common way to think about risk is in terms of likelihood – high or low? – and impact – high or low? If a risk is unlikely to happen and its impact is low, then you can probably safely ignore it. If a risk is very likely to happen and the impact would be high, you had better take lots of action. Virtually all climate scientists rate the likelihood of dangerous climate change as high and the impact as high. The only uncertainty is in the timescale. If you're in it for the short term, you can probably ignore the effects of climate change on your business; but if you're in it for the medium and longer term, the sooner you take action, the more controllable that risk will be.

Very few businesses are completely ignoring energy price rises and climate change. Many businesses are simply reacting to events. If energy becomes more expensive, we'll tell staff to turn off the lights. If we get an unusually hot summer, we'll hire a few more air conditioners. Sometimes a highly reactive strategy is quite a good one for business – there's something to be said for being agile and changing as you need to. In the case of the low-carbon economy, however, this is usually a poor strategy. Because the implications and timescales of energy and climate change are so big and long, there are some decisions you need to take now if you're to remain competitive in five or ten years' time. These decisions often require an upfront capital investment.

For these reasons, an increasing number of businesses are taking a proactive stance on energy prices and climate change: they're taking action now to guarantee long-term success. Proactive businesses are taking action in five main areas: managing energy, managing carbon, mitigation, becoming sustainable, and creating new products and services.

Managing energy means reducing both your overall energy usage and your reliance on fossil fuels.

Managing carbon means measuring and reducing the greenhouse gases your company produces, not only in its immediate operations but throughout the supply chain.

Mitigation means taking action now to ensure that your company can continue to thrive as the climate changes.

Sustainability means creating a business that doesn't provide for today's generation at the expense of future generations.

Creating new products and services means harnessing your company's skills and assets to the kind of products and services people will buy as the economy changes.

There are two reasons for taking action in this way. The first is selfish – companies that are proactive now will be more prosperous than those that don't. They'll be more competitive because they've reduced costs and increased revenues. As Walmart CEO Lee Scott observed:

> As we look at our responsibility as one of the world's largest companies, it just became obvious that sustainability was an issue that was going to be more important …. As I got exposed to the opportunities we had

to reduce our impact, it became even more exciting than I had originally thought: It is clearly good for our business. We are taking costs out and finding we are doing things we just do not need to do, whether it be in packaging, or energy usage, or the kind of equipment we buy for refrigeration in our stores. There are a number of decisions we can make that are great for sustainability and great for bottom-line profit.

The second reason is more altruistic. The products and services businesses offer have improved the quality of life of billions of people throughout the world – its businesses operating in a free market economy that has enabled billions of us alive today to enjoy a standard of living that even a king would have envied less than a hundred years ago. But it's precisely those businesses and their products that have used up so much fossil fuel, putting CO_2 and other greenhouse gases into the atmosphere, that threaten to destroy part or all of this astonishing standard of living that so many of us enjoy today. In fact, it's worse than that, because climate change will have a disproportionately negative effect on some of the world's poorest people. We may have to drive less – they will starve.

But businesses can change that. By using energy in a different way, and by developing new business models and new products and services, businesses can not only halt climate change, but even reverse it – while continuing to ensure that even more of the world's 7 billion people can share in standard of living that a free market economy can bring. To put if more bluntly, business has got us into this mess – it's the responsibility of business to get us out of it. Terry Leahy, then boss of Tesco, summed this up this in a 2007 speech:

We now know that the implications of climate change are huge. I am not a scientist. But I listen when the scientists say that, if we fail to mitigate climate change, the environmental, social and economic consequences will be stark and severe. This has profound implications for all of us, for our children, and for our children's children.

For each one of us this poses a challenge. What role are we to play? Passive or active? Follower or leader? There comes a moment when it is clear what you must do. I am determined that Tesco should be a leader in helping to create a low-carbon economy.

In saying this, I do not underestimate the task. It is to take an economy where human comfort, activity and growth are inextricably linked with emitting carbon. And to transform it into one which can only thrive without depending on carbon. This is a monumental challenge. It requires a revolution in technology and a revolution in thinking. We are going to have to re-think the way we live and work.

Most business leaders are driven by a complex set of often highly idiosyncratic motives, but it's common for two key factors to play a part. Most business people like to be successful, and as money makes a convenient scorecard, that often means that business leaders like to make plenty of money. But most business leaders also like to feel they're making some kind of contribution – that in some ways they're leaving a worthwhile legacy of some kind.

Being proactive about the low-carbon economy enables you to create a business that is not only profitable, but one that also helps, in some small way, to make the world a better place. Why wouldn't you want to do that?

PART II

The Features of the Low-carbon Economy

We know that the cost of fossil fuel energy will rise, although we don't know how fast and by how much. We know that climate change will make the world warmer, though we don't know just how severe the effects of warming will be, or how quickly they'll happen. What does all this mean for you and your business?

Some changes are certain: we'll have to develop low-carbon forms of energy; we'll have to be more energy-efficient, and we'll have to develop low-carbon forms of transport. In the next three chapters we'll we explore each of these three features of the low-carbon economy.

Some changes are much less predictable: no one knows whether skyrocketing energy prices will lead to global recession and conflict, or whether new technologies will give us cheaper energy and renewed economic growth; no one knows whether climate change will turn out to be so gradual that we can easily adapt to it, or whether its effects will oblige us to structure our economies and live our lives in radically different ways.

Just because something is uncertain is no reason not to take action, and in Part III of this book we'll use the powerful technique of scenario planning to consider what might happen, in order to prepare your business for an uncertain future.

But first we'll look at the three things we can be sure about, because they're already happening: the move towards low-carbon energy, more energy efficiency and low-carbon transport.

4

Low-carbon Energy

Not only will atomic power be released, but someday we will harness the rise and fall of the tides and imprison the rays of the sun.

Thomas Edison, inventor, in 1921

A medium-sized industrial country like the UK gets through a lot of electricity. On average, the nation is using about 40GW. At peak times this rises to about 63GW. Where does all this power come from?

In 2010 47 per cent came from gas-fired power stations. A typical gas-fired power station produces 0.5GW, though most are smaller and a few are larger. Coal-fired power stations provided 28 per cent, with a typical power station providing 1GW. Nuclear accounted for 16 per cent, with 1GW again being the typical size, and renewable energy delivered 7 per cent, mainly wind and hydroelectric. The other 2 per cent was a mixture of oil-fired power and imports.

As we move towards the low-carbon economy, this mix will change. Gas-fired power stations will probably stay with us for some time. Coal-fired power stations will close relatively rapidly, though some may be converted to biomass, and others may be rebuilt with carbon capture and storage. Most of the UK's existing nuclear power stations are coming to the end of their working life anyway, so will need to be replaced either by new nuclear power stations or by renewables. And the share of renewable energy, currently 7 per cent, will need to increase very rapidly indeed. What will that look like?

Wind

The biggest increase in renewable energy in the UK, at least in the short term, will come from wind power. Wind is a technology we are very familiar with.

On the eve of the British Industrial Revolution in the mid-eighteenth century there were over 10,000 windmills at work, mostly grinding wheat into flour. The technology of generating electricity from wind is relatively simple, and making a wind turbine is technically quite easy. Added to that, the British Isles are usually pretty windy, so it's no surprise that the doubling in renewable electricity generation in the UK since 2005 has largely been due to wind from both onshore and offshore windfarms. Windfarms are relatively cheap to construct (at least on land) and require no fuel: once they're operational, the power is essentially free.

That's the good news; now for the bad. Windfarms have two major drawbacks. First, fairly obviously, the wind doesn't blow all the time. The average power generated by a windfarm depends on its location: in the Shetlands, where the wind is generally pretty strong and constant, the average output is about 60 per cent of the peak power rating; in the south of England it drops to less than 10 per cent. A typical figure for an onshore windfarm is 30 per cent. The second, less obvious, drawback is that it takes quite a large area covered with wind turbines to produce quite a modest amount of power.

The UK's largest onshore windfarm is at Whitlee, near Glasgow in Scotland, which covers an area of 55 square kilometres. It produces a peak of 322MW, or an average of about 100MW. That's about a tenth of the output of an average coal-fired power station. If you wanted to generate all the UK's electricity from wind, you'd need about 800 windfarms like Whitlee, which would cover an area bigger than Wales.

The alternative to land-based windfarms is offshore wind. The advantages of offshore are that the wind tends to blow more regularly and people generally don't object to the turbines spoiling the view. The disadvantages are that it's much more expensive to build and maintain the turbines, and it's more expensive to transmit the electricity to where people want it. The UK's largest offshore windfarm is near Thanet, in Kent, where it covers an area of 35 square kilometres, and its maximum capacity is 300MW, or about one third that of a typical coal-fired power station. Offshore wind is a growing area. In January 2010 the British government granted licences to develop nine huge offshore windfarms with a total peak capacity of 32GW, giving an average power supply of about 11GW, or one eighth of the country's total electricity needs.

What about when the wind doesn't blow? The country with the most experience of wind power is Denmark, which has a peak capacity of 3GW, producing on average 660MW of power, or about 20 per cent of its total electricity consumption. How do they cope with the fickle Scandinavian winds? Norway, next door to Denmark, generates almost all its electricity from hydroelectric power stations. When the wind blows in Denmark, Norway turns off some of its hydro power and imports wind-generated electricity from its neighbour. When the wind doesn't blow in Denmark, Norway opens up a few more valves and the Danes import Norwegian hydro power.

The UK has the capacity to do something similar, albeit on a much smaller scale. In particular, the UK has four pump storage power stations, one of which is built almost entirely inside a mountain at Dinorwig in North Wales. When demand for electricity it high, water flows from Marchlyn Mawr reservoir and generates a maximum of 1.2GW. When demand for electricity is low, electricity is used to pump that water back up to the top of the mountain again. Fluctuations in wind could be balanced by pump storage hydroelectric power.

Wind power will be an important part of the energy mix, especially in blustery countries like Britain, but it will never come anywhere near supplying the total electricity needs of even a small industrialised country.

Water

Water power, like wind power, has been around for a long time. About 6,000 watermills are recorded in the Domesday Book, William the Conqueror's 1086 inventory of his newly acquired kingdom. The UK currently generates slightly over 1 per cent of its energy from hydroelectric power, but this is unlikely to increase by very much despite the attractiveness of hydroelectricity. This is partly because conventional hydroelectric plants don't produce that much power. The UK's biggest conventional hydroelectric plant at Mossford in Scotland produces a measly 250MW, and most UK hydro installations are in the 2–40MW range. But it's mainly because all the good sites have already been used up. The only significant hydro power stations to be built in the UK since the Second World War have been pump storage schemes like Dinorwig in Wales, where the water is stored not primarily behind huge dams, but in a high-level lake, which is replenished (usually at nighttime) by pumping the water back up to it again.

This lack of suitable sites is true for most of Europe, but not for the rest of the world. Globally, almost 20 per cent of all electricity comes from hydroelectric power. The world's biggest hydro plant is the Itaipu Dam on the Brazil–Paraguay border. It generates 14GW – enough to meet 95 per cent of Paraguay's (admittedly fairly modest) electricity needs, and 20 per cent of Brazil's. When it's fully operational, the Three Gorges Dam on the Yangtse River in China will generate 22GW – a third of the UK's total current electricity needs, but only 3 per cent of China's. Really big projects like the Three Gorges tend to be quite unpopular because they require the flooding of huge areas of land: 1.3 million people were rehoused for the construction of the Three Gorges Dam, and that's probably only possible in an autocratic country headed by a president who used to work for a hydroelectric power company.

We're unlikely to see any more conventional, large-scale hydroelectric plants being built in the UK, or for that matter, Europe or the USA, any time soon. The growth areas, and the business opportunities, will be for unconventional hydro – small-scale, wave, and tidal.

In the UK there are currently 20 micro-hydroelectric schemes in operation, with another 50 planned. Settle Community Hydro, based in a small Yorkshire town, is typical, generating 50kW, or enough power to supply around 60 homes. China already has more than 85,000 small-scale hydroelectric plants.

Another way to generate power from water is through waves and tides. Despite Scotland's First Minister Alex Salmond's claim in 2010 that Scotland would become the Saudi Arabia of marine energy, there are, in 2012, no commercially operational wave or tidal power plants off the coast of Scotland or anywhere else in the British Isles. However, there are scores of companies trying to get it to work, ranging from underwater flaps and turbines to floating articulated snakes. If successful, each installation could provide 500MW or so, and make a modest contribution to the UK's energy needs.

Biomass

Throughout most of human history, people cooked and kept themselves warm by burning wood. Even today biomass – burning wood and other non-fossil fuels – is a major energy source for people in developing countries, and it's making a comeback in the developed world too. Biomass comes in three varieties.

Variety one is burning wood in a conventional way, either to produce heat or to boil water for steam to turn generators and produce electricity. The UK currently has one commercial wood-fired power station at Wilton, near Middlesbrough. It produces 30MW of electricity and 10MW of heat for an industrial site.

Biomass variety two is to burn stuff – usually waste products of some kind – in a slightly more complicated way to produce heat and gas. There are about 30 commercial biomass plants in the UK, mainly burning rubbish, and plans to build more. Around 9 per cent of the UK's municipal waste is currently incinerated, with most of the heat used to generate electricity.

Biomass variety three uses waste products to generate heat and power through a process known as anaerobic digestion. Waste organic products – from food to excrement – are allowed to decompose in an oxygen-free container. In so doing, they produce methane gas, which can be burnt to produce heat and power. The residual sludge can be used as a fertiliser. An anaerobic digestion facility attached to a sewage farm near Didcot produces gas which supplies 200 nearby homes. In theory, an anaerobic digestion facility attached to every sewage treatment plant in the country could supply gas to 350,000 homes.

Geothermal Energy

You only need to go 5 kilometres or so beneath the Earth's surface to find rocks hot enough to boil water. If you can drill a suitable borehole, inject water into the hot layer, and bring it back to the surface as hot water or steam, you have a wonderful free, renewable source of energy.

In practice, it's a lot more tricky, and although there are geothermal power plants in 24 countries producing more than 10GW in total, they tend to be sited in places where the naturally occurring geology drives hot rock or naturally occurring hot water closer to the surface. Iceland, which is favoured with such geology, produces about a quarter of its electricity in this way. A pilot project in Newcastle upon Tyne, in the North of England, hopes to tap into naturally occurring hot water 2 kilometres below the site of an old brewery in order to heat a new science park. However, unless there are major technological breakthroughs in drilling deep underground, geothermal energy is unlikely to become a major source of renewable energy except in a few geologically quirky spots.

Solar

Wind, water, biomass and geothermal energy all have a contribution to make to the world's energy supplies, but in most cases their contribution will be relatively modest. If we're serious about renewable energy, one source shines out above all others – solar power.

Every second, 4 million tonnes of hydrogen is transformed into helium in the massive nuclear reactor we call the Sun, and although it's 93 million miles away, enough of that energy hits the ground in the form of sunlight to power the world's total energy needs 5,000 times over. The only problem is how to capture that energy and use it.

There are two ways to produce electricity from the Sun. The first is to use a photovoltaic cell, to generate electricity directly. The technology has been around for a while on a small scale, but remains quite expensive. In bright sunlight, 1 square metre of high-quality semiconductors will produce about 150W of power. This isn't a huge amount of power – enough to light three traditional incandescent lightbulbs – but if you have the space to set out plenty of panels, you can generate a fair amount of power. The world's largest solar photovoltaic power station is in Arizona, where some 5 million panels generate around 300MW of power. The plant's owners, First Solar, are building two more plants in California with a capacity of 550MW.

As a result of government subsidies, mainly in the form of Feed-in Tariffs where solar panel owners are paid for the electricity they generate, there has been a worldwide boom in solar photovoltaic panel production. This has not only driven new technologies, but also driven down the price. In the USA, solar power now costs around $120 per megawatt hour, in comparison with around $70 for offshore wind and gas-fired power stations. But as the technology advances and economies of scale kick in, solar power – in sunny countries at least – will soon be the most economical form of power. This is especially the case in India, China, Africa and the Middle East. In India, for example, more than 7GW of electricity is provided from standalone diesel generators at a cost of around $250 per megawatt hour, so solar is already highly competitive.

Sadly, solar power is not so effective in cloudy northern European countries like the UK. Even Germany, which has been encouraging solar power for many years with FITs, only manages to generate 1 per cent of its electricity from solar power, mainly from a very large number of domestic installations. Its biggest commercial system, at Finsterwalde, can manage 80MW on a really hot summer day.

But photovoltaics are not the only way to generate power from the Sun. You can simply use the Sun's rays to heat water. A typical domestic system consists of a few square metres of tightly packed black piping that sits on your roof and feeds hot water into the system. Even in the colder, gloomier north of England, a typical system can provide about half the hot water used by a family of four. In hotter, sunnier countries, this approach to solar power has a lot of potential.

Taking this concept a step further, why not use mirrors to concentrate the energy of the Sun and use it to boil water? You can then use the resultant steam to drive a turbine, a generator and produce electricity. This is exactly what happens in a concentrated solar power (CSP) station. If your country happens to have a lot of sunlight, CSP makes a lot of sense. The world's largest CSP station is in the Mojave Desert in California, and it generates 350MW. In 2010 there was about 1GW of concentrated solar power in action, with another 14GW due to come online in the next few years. The designs vary a bit – some have curved mirrors focusing the Sun's rays onto a collector at the top of a tower; others have fields of parabolic trough mirrors, beaming the sunlight onto long tubes which run through the troughs. Some heat up the water directly, some use the sunlight to heat molten salt which is then used to boil the steam for the generators. Molten salt holds its temperature quite well, so the power station can produce through the night when the Sun doesn't shine.

Why not build some really big solar thermal power stations in North Africa, where it's sunny a lot of the time, and send the electricity to Europe? This is the aim of the Desertec Foundation. Its proposal is to build large CSP stations throughout North Africa and the Middle East, and transmit the power to Europe through high-voltage direct current cables (which lose much less energy in transmission than cables carrying alternating current). Covering 2,500 square metres of desert with CSP could provide 100GW of power – enough to supply all of Britain's energy needs with plenty to spare. While 2,500 kilometres is quite a large area of land, it's less than half of the area flooded to create a reservoir for the Aswan High Dam in Egypt – and that generates only 3GW of power. As well as solving Europe's energy problems, it would also provide a source of income for the countries in the Middle East and North African region.

How Renewables Add Up

If you want to generate power from renewable sources, wind, water, biomass, geothermal and solar are pretty much all you have to choose from. In countries with abundant sunlight, solar could solve most of their energy problems, and in countries with lots of mountains and few people, hydroelectric will probably be the answer. But for the UK, and most European countries, no single source of renewable energy is going to replace that lovely, abundant, cheap power we get from burning coal and gas.

So how will energy generation pan out in the low-carbon economy in these countries? First, there'll need to be a multiplicity of sources. We'll need wind, water, solar and biomass. In the past, we've tended to rely on relatively few large sources of power – typically coal-fired power stations generating 1GW or more. In future, we'll rely on very large numbers of small generators – domestic solar PV generating 4kW, community hydro with 50kW, some large windfarms chipping in 100MW, and perhaps a big biomass power station providing 300MW.

As more renewables come into use, the price will come down and the technology will advance. It's possible in ten years' time that we'll have huge supplies of power from some technological advance we can only guess at – maybe you'll be able to power your warehouse with cheap photovoltaic cells painted on to the roof, or maybe breakthroughs in wave power will lead to a renaissance in British sea power. But until then, we can only do three things. One is to try a lot of different renewables technologies and see which ones turn out to work best and most cheaply. The second is to be more efficient with the energy we've got, the subject of the next chapter. The third is to overcome our hangups about the atom and embrace nuclear power.

Nuclear

Back in the early 1970s most of France's power stations ran on oil. When world oil prices quadrupled in 1974, the French government made a key strategic decision: as an industrial country with few natural resources, it would find a way to generate its power independent of oil and gas from the Middle East and coal from Germany. It would develop its own nuclear power industry. France opened its first nuclear power plant in 1965, and now has about 60 nuclear reactors generating around 500 terrawatt hours (TWh) each year. As well as providing cheap electricity for the French, France exports about 100TWh to other European countries, including Britain.

The technology of nuclear power is fairly straightforward. You take a lump of uranium-235 and fire a proton into it. This creates uranium-236, which, being unstable, splits into two smaller atoms (of barium and krypton) while releasing two spare neutrons and a lot of heat. Those spare neutrons bash into other pieces of uranium-235, and off we go again – hence the term chain reaction. In an atomic bomb the whole thing is designed to spin out of control and produce a lot of energy very quickly, but in a power station it is, apparently, quite easy to keep things at a suitable pace without anything too sinister happening. The process uses no fossil fuels and produces no carbon dioxide. Although it's quite expensive to build a nuclear power station, the running costs are low and the electricity you produce is comparable in price to that of a coal-, gas- or oil-fired power station. Nuclear power stations do produce radioactive waste that needs to be stored carefully, and this isn't a trivial issue, but overall, nuclear power seems to provide the answer to all our energy needs. So why are so few nuclear power stations being built?

March 1979 saw the release of a film called *The China Syndrome*, which depicted an accident at a nuclear power plant which threatened to contaminate and render uninhabitable 'an area the size of Pennsylvania'. Twelve days after the film's release a real nuclear power plant at Three Mile Island in Pennsylvania suffered an accident similar to that in the film, and although no one was killed or seriously injured, the incident reinforced the perception that nuclear power was extremely dangerous. Fast-forward to 1986, and an accident in the Chernobyl nuclear power plant did contaminate and render uninhabitable an area of some 3,000 square kilometres, which, while only 2.5 per cent of the area of Pennsylvania, was enough to convince most people that nuclear power was just too dangerous to be trusted.

The facts are somewhat different. From 1986 until 2010 there have been 443 nuclear power stations producing 16 per cent of the entire world's electricity with no significant accidents. The World Health Organisation estimates that a total of 4,000 people will eventually die prematurely as a result of the Chernobyl disaster. While this is a terrible toll, more than 4,000 miners die every year in Chinese coal mines. It's also estimated that 24,000 people die every year as a result of pollution from coal-fired power stations.

In the early years of the twenty-first century, as concerns about climate change and energy security increased, the tide began to turn once more in favour of nuclear power. In 2008 the then Labour government in the UK approved plans to construct ten new nuclear power stations. Many prominent environmentalists – notably James Lovelock, whose Gaia Theory influenced a whole generation of green thinkers – came out in favour of nuclear power.

Then, in March 2011, an underwater earthquake triggered a huge tsunami that killed at least 16,000 and destabilised a nuclear power plant at Fukushima in Japan. Although there have as yet been no deaths directly attributable to the partial meltdown in Fukushima's six American-designed reactors, the event has reignited concerns about nuclear safety, and caused at least one government – Germany – to accelerate the closure of existing nuclear plants. The upshot of all this is that not only is nuclear power as controversial as ever, but the costs of constructing new plants will increase as a result of increased political risk.

Although no one knows how the arguments about nuclear power will eventually be resolved, the most likely outcome is that governments throughout the world will, in the main, quietly continue to approve the construction of new plants. This may not always be politically popular, but it's certainly more popular than running out of generating capacity and imposing power cuts.

Carbon Capture and Storage

If we can't ramp up our supplies of renewable energy fast enough, and we can't build nuclear power stations fast enough, we have one last card to play in the power generation stakes – carbon capture and storage (CCS). The basic principle of CCS is very simple: generate power by burning coal, but instead of allowing all that CO_2 to escape into the atmosphere, capture it and store it somewhere safely – probably underground. In practice, it's a bit more tricky. You can't just stick some gigantic CO_2 filter on top of a conventional coal-fired plant, so you have to burn the coal in a different way. One method is to burn coal in pure oxygen rather than air, and this makes capturing the CO_2 easier. Unfortunately, it takes a lot of energy to do this, and so reduces the output of the plant by anything between a quarter and a half. Once you've done this, you have to find a safe place to store the CO_2 – probably a saline aquifer deep underground. This means you have to transport the CO_2 there and make sure it doesn't escape. There's currently one 'demonstration' CCS coal-fired power station in the UK, in Renfrew, Scotland, and it generates 40MW. Given that

40 per cent of all the electricity in the world is generated by burning coal, you'd think that quite a lot of effort would have gone into CCS research, but the results of what little research has been done have been disappointing. Technologically, it's all possible, but no one has yet found a feasible way to perform carbon capture and storage at scale, in a cost-effective way. In 2007 the UK government launched a competition to build a British CCS plant, but by 2011 there was only one contender for the position, at Longannet in Scotland. Building the plant would cost £1 billion, and operating it more than £100 million a year – not including the cost of storing the captured carbon. This price tag was too much for a cash-strapped UK government, and it withdrew its offer of funding in November 2011.

Other countries may be willing to make this kind of investment in CCS, or there may be some technological breakthrough that will change the economics of carbon capture, but for now it appears that CCS is destined to be a bit of red herring in the low-carbon economy.

5

Energy Efficiency

This may sound too good to be true, but the U.S. has a renewable-energy resource that is perfectly clean, remarkably cheap, surprisingly abundant and immediately available. It has astounding potential to reduce the carbon emissions that threaten our planet, the dependence on foreign oil that threatens our security and the energy costs that threaten our wallets. Unlike coal and petroleum, it doesn't pollute; unlike solar and wind, it doesn't depend on the weather; unlike ethanol, it doesn't accelerate deforestation or inflate food prices; unlike nuclear plants, it doesn't raise uncomfortable questions about meltdowns or terrorist attacks or radioactive-waste storage, and it doesn't take a decade to build. It isn't what-if like hydrogen, clean coal and tidal power; it's already proven to be workable, scalable and cost-effective. And we don't need to import it. This miracle juice goes by the distinctly boring name of energy efficiency.
Michael Grunwald, Senior Correspondent, TIME *Magazine*

Although alternative sources of energy will play a big part in the low-carbon economy, it's unlikely that renewables and nuclear will be developed quickly enough or cheaply enough to meet our growing energy needs. For this reason, a major feature of the low-carbon economy will be the need to be much more efficient with the energy we do use.

In the UK, as in most industrialised countries, roughly a third of all energy use is by industry, a third is domestic, and a third is transport. In this chapter we'll focus on energy efficiency by businesses and homes, and in the next chapter we'll look at transport.

Buildings

Nowhere are we more profligate in energy than the way we heat and power our homes, offices, stores and factories. About a third of all the energy we use in the UK is used for heating.

Strictly speaking, it's not necessary to heat some buildings at all. It's perfectly possible to construct a building so well insulated that it requires no source of heat other than the body heat of the people who inhabit it. The concept, originally from Germany, is often described as Passiv Haus. There are probably about 20,000 buildings in the world built to Passiv Haus standards, including a student hall of residence in Leeds and a local government offices in Powys, Wales.

While Passiv Haus buildings will remain rare for some time to come, standards of insulation and energy efficiency in new buildings will continue to rise as we move further into the low-carbon economy.

BedZED, the Beddington Zero Emission Development in South London, is a community of 99 homes and managed workspaces built to encourage a low-carbon lifestyle. The houses use 80 per cent less energy to heat, and 50 per cent less electricity, than a conventional house, and much of this power is generated locally from solar panels. While such developments are still unusual in 2012, they will become increasingly common.

While it's easier to construct a new building in a highly energy-efficient way, it's also possible to reduce energy costs by 'retro-fitting' an existing building. Energy performance certificates were introduced for buildings in 2008, where A is the best and G the worst. Around 17 per cent of all UK homes are graded F and G. For a cost of around £3,000 most of these F and G grade homes could be transformed into E grade or higher with loft and cavity wall insulation and better heating systems.

Most houses in the UK are heated by gas, at a cost (in 2011) of around £1,000 per year. But there's a much more efficient system – a heat pump. The most efficient heat pump on the market in 2010 could heat the same house using electricity at a cost of just £700 a year. So how do they work, and what's the catch?

You probably already have a heat pump installed in your house: it's called a fridge. A typical refrigerator transfers heat from the inside of an insulated box to a panel on the outside (which is why those bits of wire and tubing on the back of your fridge feel warm). A heat pump simply transfers heat from outside the house and warms up the inside. It can transfer heat from the air outside (an air source heat pump) or the ground outside (a ground source heat pump). What isn't intuitively obvious is that this is a fantastically efficient way of heating a building. One unit of electricity can produce 1kWh of heat if used to power a standard electric fire, but it can produce 4kWh of heat if used in a heat pump, making heat pumps four times as efficient as an electric fire. They are also much more efficient than gas central heating.

So what's the catch? Why don't more people use heat pumps? Well, in many European countries they do – in Germany, for example, 20 per cent of domestic dwellings are warmed by heat pumps. The problem is the upfront cost. A heat pump system for a typical three-bedroom house might cost £10,000, compared to £2,000 for a typical gas central heating boiler.

Many forms of energy efficiency, from heat pumps to loft insulation, require an upfront investment in order to reap the long-term benefits, and when cash is tight, people are unwilling or unable to make that investment. This is likely to change, partly as a result of rising energy prices making the investments more attractive, and partly through innovative financing schemes which enable people to borrow the upfront costs and repay later as their energy bills are reduced.

We don't just heat our homes – we also light them, and use an increasing range of energy-hungry devices, from cookers and fridges to TVs and mobile phone chargers. As we move into the low-carbon economy, energy-efficient lighting will replace traditional incandescent bulbs. Compact fluorescent bulbs, which use about a quarter the energy of a traditional lightbulb, will gradually give way to LED-based lighting, which uses around a tenth of the power of an incandescent. Although we'll doubtless want to bring even more gadgets and devices into our homes, those devices will become more energy-efficient. Some flat-screen TVs use a third of the power of a traditional cathode ray tube box; a modern refrigerator uses a quarter less electricity than the average fridge of ten years ago.

Businesses will also become more energy-efficient. One of Tesco's newest stores, in Cheetham Hill, Manchester, uses 50 per cent less energy than a typical supermarket thanks to high levels of insulation, natural ventilation, a lighting system that automatically dims when natural light it strong, and energy-efficient refrigeration. The Co-operative Group's new head office building in Manchester will halve its current head office energy costs.

Although energy-efficient offices, stores and factories will be a key feature of the low-carbon economy, another kind of change will have at least as great an impact in reducing energy bills – the move towards flexible working.

Flexible Working

Every day in the UK, about 30 million people go to work. They walk, cycle, take a bus, train or car from their home to their workplace. At the end of their working day, they come back again. About half of these people need to be in a particular place to do their job – they serve in a shop, use equipment in a factory or drive a delivery van. But about half simply go to an office.

Or at least they used to. Increasing numbers of formerly office-based staff now work flexibly. Instead of going to their own desk at the office every day, they do some combination of working from home, 'hotdesking' at any convenient location office, and mobile working – that is to say, working from a car, a train or even a local coffee shop.

Not everyone likes the idea of flexible working. Staff feel that they'll miss the social interaction of being with others at work, and managers are unsure about how they can trust people to do a good job when they can't see them. Nevertheless, flexible working will continue as a trend and will be a key feature of the low-carbon economy – and here's why.

From the employer's point of view, it's a great way of saving money and increasing productivity. Telecoms giant BT, which has 16,000 of its workforce based at home, reckons that home working saves it £6,000 per person per year in office costs, while increasing individual productivity by 20 per cent and decreasing absenteeism. Flexible working drives managers to manage more effectively, because of the increased focus on delivering results rather than simply being present in the office.

There are potentially even bigger gains for employees. The average UK commute is 45 minutes per day – time that's rarely enjoyable or productive. About 10 million people drive to work each day, with an average round trip of 15 miles a day. This will cost something around between £1,000 and £3,000 a year, depending on the type of car and any parking charges. Those who commute to work by train pay even more, with most season tickets into London costing £2,000–4,000.

Flexible working usually leads to an increase in control over one's personal working life and better work–life balance.

In 2010 there were about 1.3 million homeworkers and a further 3.7 million who sometimes worked from home or used home as their base. Each year another 150,000 people or so become home-based, and this trend is likely to increase as employers reap the savings and employees realise the personal benefits. According to a 2009 CBI survey, 61 per cent of private sector organisations and 75 per cent of public sector organisations already have some kind of flexible working or are considering how best to implement it.

As Lynda Gratton observes in her book *The Shift: The Future of Work Is Already Here*, the key enabler of this change is technology. Ten years ago we were still pretty impressed with email and websites: today we can store information on a remote server 'in the cloud' and easily access it from anywhere. A host of cheap, easy-to-use technology tools enable us to communicate, make connections, share information and track progress. In another ten years' time it seems probable that technology will make it even easier to do work at a distance, by which time flexible working will be the norm for everyone.

The Rise of the Smart Grid

Plugging an electrical appliance into a socket and expecting a cheap, reliable source of electricity to flow is such a common part of life in the twenty-first century that it's easy to forget how recently this has all come about. Although electricity was commercially produced from the start of the twentieth century, even in 1920 less than a quarter of British homes had access to electricity because there was no national transmission system. It was Prime Minister Stanley Baldwin who promoted the idea of producing a nationally owned infrastructure for linking together the then privately owned power stations and delivering the electricity to homes and businesses. Work began in 1926, and the grid became fully operational as a national system in 1938. It cost something in the region of £1.5 billion in today's money.

The national grid is a great idea. It also allows the production of electricity to be matched by its use. You can't store electricity, at least not directly, so the grid also allows the amount of power produced to equal the amount of power used. In the UK the national grid attempts to predict demand, month by month, week by week and hour by hour. Fluctuations are managed by having more power stations operational in the winter than in the summer, and more operational in the early evening than in the small hours of the morning. This is trickier than it seems: much of the demand is weather-related and therefore hard to predict. You can't just switch a power station on and off: a coal-fired power station takes many hours to go from cold to being able to generate power, and a nuclear station takes days. Power from renewables is even more problematic – when the wind doesn't blow (or blows too hard), a windfarm produces no energy at all. When you add in accidents and equipment failures, it's remarkable that the power supply in the UK is as reliable as it is. The last major interruption to the UK supply was back in 2003, when two equipment faults led to a loss of power to 410,000 people in South London, although power was restored to most of them in under an hour. An equipment fault a week earlier in the USA had plunged several million homes and businesses into darkness, and power wasn't fully restored for several weeks. Part of the reason we've had so few blackouts in the UK is that at any given time, a number of power stations are kept on 'spinning reserve' – not actually generating power, but with all their turbines powered up and ready to generate at short notice if required.

For all its successes, the current national grid fails in two respects. Firstly, it's geared up to be largely one-way – transmitting power from relatively few big power stations (about 180 in the UK in 2010) to millions of individual homes and businesses. Secondly, it conveys power, but not information.

A smart grid, by contrast, would be both a two-way system and a conveyor of information. Here's how it would work.

To begin with, it would allow for hundreds of thousands of small-scale electricity generators to feed into the grid – domestic solar photovoltaics, small-scale windfarms, local hydroelectric schemes and regional tidal power. The process of matching supply and demand would have to be done by the grid itself, rather than by human intervention. At the moment there's a human controller sitting in a room of the national grid who knows that when the popular British soap opera *EastEnders* finishes, 1.75 million people will ease themselves out of their armchairs and toddle into the kitchen to put on the kettle:

1.75 million kettles require about 3GW of electricity to boil – that's about the output of three medium-sized power stations. As the programme draws to an end, our grid controller taps a keyboard to tell the Dinorwig pump storage hydroelectric power station in North Wales to open the taps. Hydroelectric is chosen because it's the fastest and easiest way to turn power on and off. It's possible for humans to do this when there are only a small number of fairly easy to control sources of power – but with the spread of renewables and the increase in microgeneration, this will no longer be possible. The grid itself will have to manage this balancing act.

When you access an Internet site that happens to be based in another country, the bits and bytes of information flowing from that website to your computer don't all take the same route. Because the Internet is smart, the World Wide Web itself decides how to package up that information and which routes to send it over. You don't know and you don't care, as long as it arrives quickly and correctly. In an analogous way, a smart grid will balance the flow of electricity from wherever it's provided to wherever it's needed, and the way it will do this is by providing information as well as power.

At the moment, each unit of electricity costs pretty much the same as any other (with the exception of some economy tariffs that allow you to pay less for electricity at night when demand is lower). But imagine that the cost of electricity varied from minute to minute, according to demand and supply, and imagine that information on the cost of electricity was transmitted along with the power itself. Now imagine that every device that uses electricity is able to tell how much electricity it's using and react accordingly. Then you have a smart grid.

Some devices would stay on all the time, irrespective of how much electricity costs. It's no use having a television that switches itself off in the middle of your favourite programme just because a lot of other people are watching it too. But many devices would switch themselves on and off selectively. You could load your washing machine or tumble drier and tell it to operate only when electricity was cheap; your fridge freezer, which in any case uses electricity only intermittently, could switch itself off for a while when the price was high, and chargers for laptops and other mobile devices could switch on only when the price was low. Perhaps most significantly of all, the batteries in your electric car would not only recharge themselves only when electricity was cheap, they could actually provide electricity to the grid when the price was high.

A smart grid has three significant advantages. Firstly, it would reduce overall electricity consumption by making devices and their owners aware of the cost of electricity. Secondly, it would allow for alternative sources of power generation, especially from micro-generation and renewables. Thirdly, it would reduce the peak demand for electricity, therefore significantly reducing the overall cost of the country's energy infrastructure.

The basic components of a smart grid are already in place – conveying information through power lines, managing supply and demands automatically, providing real-time information on the energy usage of individual electrical equipment. What's needed now is to integrate them together, and pilots are already under way to test the concept in Austin, Texas, Mannheim in Germany and Evora in Portugal. Smart grids will make a major contribution to energy efficiency in the low-carbon economy.

6

Low-carbon Transport

In twenty years, all cars will be electric.

Warren Buffett, investor, in 2009

In 2012, the world uses about 88 million barrels of oil every day. Fifty million of these barrels are used in transport, by a billion road vehicles, 300,000 aircraft and 50,000 large ships.

As the world population increases, and as more countries want better and faster transport, this demand can only increase: China, for example, has added another 9.5 million vehicles to the roads every year since 2006, bringing the 2012 total to over 100 million vehicles.

How will this change in the low-carbon economy? Let's start with the biggest single consumer of fossil fuels on the planet: the motor car.

Cars

Traditional cars vary enormously in their fuel consumption. While the average UK car will deliver 33 miles per gallon, a typical sports utility vehicle will do around 20 and an economy compact will deliver more than 80. Cars driven by a traditional internal combustion engine (ICE) have become significantly more fuel-efficient in the last few years. Although substantial efficiency gains are possible using existing technology, there is an inherent limit on how energy-efficient conventional internal combustion engine cars can be: in a standard petrol car, 75 per cent of the energy created is turned into heat, which is why cars need radiators. If you want to make cars more efficient and use less fossil fuel energy, there are three alternative power sources: biofuels, hydrogen and electricity.

BIOFUELS

In theory, you can make the fuel for an internal combustion engine from a wide variety of sources – sugar cane, corn, algae, cooking oil, even a mixture of waste organic material. Could this be the answer for ICE-powered vehicles?

The biggest success story for biofuel is Brazil, where half of the country's 25 million cars can run on any proportion of petrol and ethanol. It's mandatory for new vehicles to run on at least 25 per cent ethanol, and many use 100 per cent because it's cheaper than petrol. The ethanol is produced from sugar cane. The stems of the sugar cane are burnt to produce heat and electricity, which is used to distil the sugar into ethanol. Although there have been some ups and downs in the take-up of ethanol fuel, the scheme is widely considered to be a success.

The USA is very keen on biofuels. Sugar cane doesn't grow as well in the USA as it does in Brazil, so corn is used as the principal feedstock. The stems of corn don't burn the way sugar cane stems do, so the heat and electricity for the distillation process is usually provided by burning coal. Corn growing is an important activity in a number of lightly populated states, and corn ethanol production has received huge sums of subsidy from the federal government – something like $5 billion a year. Growing the corn requires large amounts of nitrogen-based fertiliser, which in turn requires large amounts of natural gas to produce; distilling it into biofuel also requires a lot of energy. The net effect is that biofuel produced in this way uses more energy and produces more greenhouse gases than conventional oil-based petrol and diesel. Even worse, using land in this way reduces its availability for crops and drives up food prices.

About 3 per cent of the fuel you put into your car from an ordinary petrol filling station in the UK is biofuel – either biodiesel or ethanol. A few years ago, European governments were quite enthusiastic about biofuels and mandated that more than 5 per cent of the fuel mix for road vehicles would be biofuel by 2010. Although the target has been missed, most of the UK's biofuel is imported, including Argentinean biodiesel based on soya. Quite apart from the competition with food crops, it makes little sense to import biofuel from across the world. Unless there are significant advances in home-grown biofuel, possible from algae or waste products, it is unlikely that biofuel will contribute significantly to road transport in the low-carbon economy.

HYDROGEN

The next option is hydrogen. Hydrogen can be used in two ways in a road vehicle. It can be burnt as a gas in an ICE, or it can be used to power a fuel cell. In both cases the emissions from the vehicle itself are zero, apart from some water vapour. Hydrogen-powered buses already operate in London, Vancouver, Perth and Reykjavik. Many motor manufacturers, including Ford and BMW, have successfully produced hydrogen fuel cell cars, which have the range and performance of a petrol-driven car, but zero tailpipe emissions. Former Governor Schwarzenegger of California drove a hydrogen-powered Hummer. And as the advocates of hydrogen are keen to say, hydrogen is not only clean, it's the most abundant element in the universe.

Despite this flurry of experimentation and enthusiasm, hydrogen power is almost certainly a complete non-starter for road vehicles, for two reasons. Firstly, it requires energy to produce hydrogen. The most common approach it to use electrolysis to separate the hydrogen from the oxygen in water. Unless you have an abundant source of carbon-free energy, making use of hydrogen as a fuel puts you back where you started. It actually uses more energy, and produces more CO_2 to burn oil or gas or coal to generate electricity, to produce hydrogen, to put into a zero-emission vehicle than it would do simply to burn oil in a conventional ICE. The second objection is that hydrogen is extremely difficult to store safely. It's prone to leak, and it's even more flammable than petrol. For these reasons, hydrogen is very unlikely to contribute significantly to road transport.

ELECTRICITY

Once you've eliminated biofuels and hydrogen from the equation, there's really only one way to go with low-carbon road transport: electricity.

If you want to buy an electric car right now, you can do so. The Tesla Roadster gives you 0–60mph in 3.9 seconds, a top speed of 125mph and a range of 200 miles for £86,750. If you're content with a range of 50 miles and a top speed of 50mph, the G-Wiz is a more modest £8,000. Another dozen companies offer models at present. When Renault launches its full range of electric cars in 2012 you'll have even more choice, from the single-seater Twizy to the Fluence family saloon.

Electric cars have a lot going for them. In terms of speed and acceleration, they perform as well or better than a conventional petrol-driven model. They are very cheap to run – the G-Wiz costs about 2p a mile to run, and in the UK is exempt from road tax. They use less energy, and produce less CO_2 emissions than a petrol or diesel car, even if the electricity they use is generated by a conventional fossil fuel power station. This is because electric motors are very efficient and the ICE is very inefficient. Perhaps most significantly, electric cars use a proven technology – electric motors – that has been around for a long time. In the early days of motoring, it was touch and go to whether petrol or electricity would be the dominant power source for the emerging motor industry. Just one thing prevents electric cars from dominating the market: batteries.

At the moment, batteries are expensive. A full set for a G-Wiz costs £1,000. Even for a car as economical as a G-Wiz, they give a range of only 50 miles. The Tesla will give you a 200-mile range, but you pay nearly £20,000 in batteries for that. Not only are batteries expensive, but they take a long time to recharge. This is fine if you use your car for short trips and you're happy to leave it plugged in overnight at home, but if you want to go on a long journey and you run out of battery charge, you're in serious trouble, even if you happen to be on one of the UK cities with a network of charging points, like London, Birmingham or Coventry.

One solution to the battery problem is not to recharge the batteries, but to replace them. A company called Better Place opened the first battery replacement stations in Denmark and Israel in 2011, to coincide with the launch of the all-electric Renault Fluence. Motorists will be able to drive into a battery replacement station (probably situated alongside a conventional petrol station) and have the batteries in their vehicle changed in less time than it takes to fill up an ordinary car with petrol. Instead of owning the batteries, motorists will pay so much per mile to use the power from them.

Although different in many ways, both Israel and Denmark are ideal countries for this experiment. Both are geographically small, with high taxes on petrol, a commitment to energy independence and a good infrastructure for electricity generation from renewables – solar in the case of Israel, wind in Denmark. Electric cars have a good chance of becoming mainstream in both places fairly soon. Just how quickly electric cars become the majority in other countries depends on how much they cost to buy and run, once you have taken into account any government subsidies, and how quickly advances in battery technology can bring down the cost.

How big will the market be? It depends on who you ask. According to 2010 research by HSBC, around 9 million new electric cars and a further 9 million plug-in hybrids will be sold in 2020 – or about a quarter of the 70 million new cars expected to be sold that year. Others are more optimistic – Better Place founder Shai Agassi expects electric cars to outsell ICE models in Israel by around 2016, and worldwide by 2020.

In a 2009 speech, investor Warren Buffett said that 'in twenty years, all cars on the road will be electric'. This was shortly after he'd bought a 10 per cent stake in Chinese electric car company BYD. This is already proving to be a shrewd investment: in 2010 the Chinese government announced that it wants to put a million electric vehicles on the road by 2015 and become the world's largest manufacturer of electric cars.

As well as seeing significantly more electric vehicles on the road in the low-carbon economy, we're likely to see a change in the ways people travel.

Currently in the UK, people use cars both for frequent short journeys (the school run, the commute to work) and for less frequent longer journeys (holidays, visiting friends, business trips). Although alternatives are available – bicycle, bus, tram, train, car sharing, hourly car rental – people tend not to use them because they're less convenient, more expensive, or both. But this might change. One scenario is that people use a small, cheap electric vehicle for their short journeys, and make other arrangements for longer ones.

For the short journeys, a partnership between General Motors and Shanghai Automotive Industry Corporation might provide a glimpse of the future. They're currently testing a kind of bubble car called an Electric Network Vehicle (ENV). At around 1.5 metres long and 1.4 metres wide, it's half the size of a Mini and can be driven manually like a conventional small car. But a sophisticated set of sensors, including GPS systems, radar to detect solid objects and infra-red sensors to detect people and animals, means that it can also drive itself. You might not want it to drive itself while on an ordinary road, but imagine the convenience if it would drop you off at the front door of a shop or office, and then go and park itself. You'd summon it back with a call from your mobile phone. The car's a two-seater, but if you wanted to bring the family along, another ENV would obligingly tag along behind the lead car.

Longer trips, you'd handle differently. You might want access to something more like a conventional car, perhaps through a car sharing or hourly rental scheme. In 2012 some 50,000 people in the UK belong to some form of car club, enabling them to access a car by the hour, and the four main UK organisations that provide this service report a doubling in membership during the last year. In 2011 the city of Paris launched a pilot of its own car club scheme, with 66 electric cars called Autolib, based on its successful Vélib bicycle sharing scheme. It intends to have more than 3,000 cars available by the end of 2012.

The other significant advantage of electric cars is that they can be used to supply power back to the grid. In the power cuts that followed the 2011 Japanese tsunami, a few enterprising owners of electric and hybrid cars used their car batteries to power small household appliances. Spotting this trend, Nissan, Toyota and Mitsubishi are all working to adapt their electric car models to provide an easy way to connect their electric cars to houses, in order to provide a backup electricity supply. As smart grids become commonplace, electric cars can act as local storage devices, raising the prospect of free motoring if motorists are able to recharge their car batteries during the night when electricity is cheap, and pay for this by selling some of it back during the day when the price is high.

Electrifying the world's fleet of cars is comparatively straightforward. The technology is pretty much there – batteries just need to get a bit better. Because most people change their cars quite regularly – every five years is the UK average – it won't take long for electric cars to form a mass market, lowering prices through economies of scale. Given that 60 per cent of all transport-based UK greenhouse gas emissions are caused by cars, electrifying this form of transport will have a big impact on both greenhouse gas emissions and energy security – though it will mean that overall demand for electricity will increase.

Trucks and Vans

Trucks and vans account for a further 30 per cent of UK transport-based greenhouse gas emissions – heavy goods vehicles 20 per cent, and light vans 10 per cent.

Vans, like cars, can be electrified, but heavy goods vehicles present more of a problem. Even if battery technology continues to advance, it seems unlikely that it will advance quickly enough to make it feasible to provide the power necessary for heavy trucks. We may see some use of biofuels, especially if they can be produced in a low-carbon way. The most important changes won't be in the way trucks are powered, but in the way they're used. Many delivery trucks travel empty, or only part-loaded, and are driven inefficiently on sub-optimal routes.

The Asda supermarket chain reduced its annual mileage by 3.4 million miles in 2009 simply by packing its lorries more efficiently. It further reduced fuel costs by remotely monitoring driver behaviour and training its drivers to be more fuel-efficient. Pharmacy chain Boots reduced its transport costs and greenhouse gas emissions by sharing deliveries with other retailers, while the Co-operative group is focusing on reducing the number of empty runs of its own fleet. Tesco has eliminated more than 15,000 lorry journeys a year by using trains to move stock between two of its main distribution depots in Daventry and Livingston.

In the low-carbon economy, while cars and vans will be electrified, heavy goods vehicles will probably continue to run on diesel. They will just be used in a more intelligent and energy-efficient way.

Trains and Buses

Trains are already a low-carbon form of transport. A standard passenger train, when full, uses only about 2.5 per cent of the energy an average petrol-driven car would use to transport a person the equivalent distance: even if the car has four occupants, the train is still only using 10 per cent of the energy the car needs. Better still, the train can easily be powered by electricity, which can be provided by non-fossil fuel sources, making the train a very low-carbon option. Part of the reason the Eurostar train service from London to Paris claims to be carbon-neutral is that its trains run on electricity mainly generated by French nuclear power.

Trains vary a great deal in their efficiency. A high-speed train like Eurostar is less than half as energy-efficient as a conventional train, and trains which are less than fully occupied become much less energy-efficient per person carried. In 2012 a healthy debate raged in the UK over the construction of HS2, a new high-speed rail line from London to Birmingham, with environmental activists on both sides of the argument: on the one hand, high-speed rail is certainly more energy-efficient and environmentally friendly than driving or flying; on the other, conventional rail is more energy-efficient and environmentally friendly than high-speed rail, especially if the initial infrastructure costs are taken into account.

Whether or not HS2 is eventually built, trains will continue to play an important part in the low-carbon economy. In 2012 the UK railway system accounts for only 2 per cent of all transport-related greenhouse gas emissions, and it's possible to extend the system with little or no impact on climate change. We can look forward to continuing expansion of the rail system. How much more depends on how quickly the alternatives rise in price and the extent to which this development is encouraged by local and national government.

Diesel-powered buses, like heavy goods vehicles, are unlikely ever to find practicable alternative sources of fuel, although trolley buses, still in use in Switzerland and some other European countries, are a possibility for some urban transport. The UK has also seen a resurgence in its urban tram network, with new tram systems in Croydon, Manchester and Nottingham. Even diesel-powered buses and coaches are considerably more energy-efficient than private cars – a full bus uses on average 8 per cent of the energy of a single-person car. Buses and coaches are likely to be an important part of the public transportation mix in the low-carbon economy.

Aircraft

A much bigger challenge is aviation. Large aircraft use about the same amount of fuel, and therefore produce similar CO_2 emissions on a passenger per mile basis, as an average car. However, there are two other factors to be taken into account. Because planes release CO_2 – and other greenhouse gases like nitrous oxides – into the stratosphere, the climate warming effect is almost double that of the same quantity of CO_2 released at ground level. Secondly, planes tend to go much further than cars. Taking both factors into account, you can produce the equivalent amount of greenhouse gases either by driving an average UK car for an average 9,000 miles a year or by taking one round trip to New York and back.

Although there have been some modest improvements in the fuel efficiency of airplanes – the 2005 A380 Superjumbo burns 12 per cent less fuel per passenger than a 35-year-old Boeing 747 – it's been nothing like the progress in the fuel efficiency of cars. Although a specially designed solar-powered plane recently stayed in the air for 24 hours, there is no prospect of commercially feasible aircraft being electrically powered, by solar panels, fuel cells, batteries or anything else. According to the laws of physics, every aircraft has to expend a certain amount of energy just to stay in the air, let alone to carry a revenue-earning payload, and energy-rich aviation fuels are really the only way to do it. If it can't be fossil fuel petrol, it'll have to be some kind of biofuel.

In 2008 a Virgin Atlantic 747 flew from London to Amsterdam partly on biofuel. To be precise, the fuel in the tank supplying one of the four engines was 80 per cent petrol and 20 per cent biofuel from coconut and babassu, a tree grown in Brazil. So it can be done, though as the 747 could have completed the flight on its other three conventional-fuelled engines, owner Richard Branson perhaps wasn't as confident as all that. But could biofuel be commercially viable? The International Air Transport Association thinks so: it has set a target for its member companies of using 10 per cent renewable source fuel by 2017. The fuel of choice is likely to be not coconut oil, but jatropha, a bushy tree that grows in tropical regions. It doesn't compete with food production or need fertiliser to grow. Weight for weight, it produces a lot of oil, and it can be mixed 50/50 with petrol to make aviation fuel.

In 2011 Virgin Atlantic made a further announcement – that it was partnering with a company called LanzaTech to recover waste gases from steel production and convert them into a low-carbon aviation fuel. It expects the first test flight using this new fuel within two to three years.

We're unlikely to see radical changes in aviation as we move towards the low-carbon economy. Some short-haul plane travel will disappear if high-speed rail offers a better alternative, as has already happened in France and Japan with well-developed high-speed rail networks. Some long-haul travel may reduce if businesses become more comfortable with videoconferencing and other communication methods, and if holidaymakers find that it's too expensive or inconvenient to travel so far. But the nature of aviation probably won't change that much. Aircraft will have to be powered by fossil fuels, though some biofuel alternatives may make a marginal difference.

Ships

Ships are already a very energy-efficient way of transporting goods: as a very rough rule of thumb, moving goods by ship requires less than a quarter of the energy needs to move it by road, and half the energy needed to move it by rail.

Nevertheless, around 5 per cent of all worldwide greenhouse gas emissions are generated by merchant ships, in part because they tend to burn a low grade of fuel known as bunker oil, which releases a lot of CO_2 and other greenhouse gases when it is burnt.

There are few realistic alternatives to oil for powering a big ship. The US Navy has committed to having half of its fleet free from oil by 2020, and it will do this with a mixture of nuclear power and biofuel. Nuclear power makes sense for very large vessels – 16 per cent of the US Navy is already nuclear-powered – but is probably uneconomic for merchant vessels. A few companies have even experimented with wind power in the form of rotary sails or even large kites, but these are unlikely ever to become mainstream.

As with heavy good vehicles, the savings in energy are likely to come from efficiencies, rather than from new fuel sources. In 2011, Danish shipping firm Maersk placed an order for ten 400-metre 'Triple E' bulk container carriers, which carry 20 per cent more cargo and produce 20 per cent less greenhouse gases than conventional bulk carriers. The energy savings result from better hull and propeller design, plus heat recovery systems to make use of the 25 per cent of energy usually lost in heat.

The simplest efficiency measure of all can apply to the world's current fleet – simply travelling more slowly would save most ships 20 per cent in energy costs.

Because it's relatively cheap to transport goods by sea, the price of fossil fuels would have to increase dramatically to have much of an impact on the world's seaborne trade. While this isn't impossible, it seems likely that in the low-carbon economy, shipping will continue to be a bit more efficient, but otherwise continue much as it is at present.

PART III

What Will it Really be Like?

Fossil fuel energy will get more expensive. The world will get warmer as burning fossil fuels and changes in land use put more greenhouse gases into the atmosphere. This much is certain. As a result, we'll use more renewable and non-fossil fuel energy, we'll be more energy-efficient, and we'll move towards low-carbon transport, especially for cars. This, too, is certain to happen – indeed, it already is happening.

But how quickly will the price of energy rise, and how severe will the effects of climate change be? What will the world be like when these effects really kick in? Will an energy crunch and runaway global warming lead to starvation, conflict and the premature death of millions, as some predict? Or will new technologies show up just in time to enable all of us to live an even more affluent lifestyle in future? Perhaps the exhaustion of natural resources will cause a fundamental reassessment in how we live, with a renewed focus on quality of life and wellbeing instead of aggressive economic growth?

The truth is, nobody knows. It's impossible to predict. Actually, it's worse than that. As Dan Gardener explained so elegantly in this book *Future Babble*, just because you can't predict the future doesn't prevent us believing people who claim they can. There's a thriving job market for economists, political advisers and journalists who claim to be able to see around the corner, even though a landmark study of 284 such experts by Philip Tetlock at the University of California demonstrated that their predictions were no better than those of a dart-throwing chimpanzee.

Just because you can't predict the future doesn't mean you can't prepare for it. The most effective technique to help you prepare for the future is scenario planning. Instead of trying to predict the future, you develop a number of possible futures, or scenarios. Understanding the consequences of the differing scenarios can help you to decide what your organisation should be doing now to prepare for them.

In the next four chapters we'll consider four possible scenarios for the low-carbon economy. In Chapter 7, 'Present Trends Continue', we'll look at how things might pan out if we carry on burning fossil fuels the way we do now, and if climate change kicks in at the rate experts think it will. In Chapter 8, 'Conflict', we'll examine how energy costs and climate change might drive a new era of conflict, both within and between nation states. In Chapter 9, 'Technology to the Rescue', we'll turn to a more optimistic scenario, in which technological advances enable us to have an even better standard of living than the one we enjoy today. Finally, in Chapter 10, 'Less Is More', we'll consider how a more frugal approach to energy use could result in a different kind of society.

Is any one of these scenarios more likely than any other? Although it's tempting to try to predict, the only thing you can say with any certainty is that present trends won't continue. Apart from that, it's impossible to tell. Only by examining a range of scenarios can you build an organisation with sufficient resilience and flexibility to withstand anything the future can throw at it.

7

Present Trends Continue

I never think of the future – it comes soon enough.
Albert Einstein, physicist

Until 2020

The 2008–2009 economic crisis determined the course of European economies for some years to come. Even as late as 2018, European economies were still growing at less than 2 per cent, while many Asian economies, particularly China, continued to grow at 8 per cent or more. In Europe and the West there was steady progress towards a low-carbon economy, with increases in renewable power generation, and gradual adoption of electric vehicles. Most Asian countries continued to achieve growth by burning lots of fossil fuels, and as a result global CO_2 emissions continued to rise.

The year 2016 brought the energy crunch. Within the space of a few months, the price of oil leapt from around $80 a barrel to more than $200 a barrel. With UK petrol priced at 260p a litre, it now cost more than £130 to fill a typical 50-litre tank of petrol. Manufacturers couldn't produce electric cars quickly enough, and people couldn't sell anything but the most economical of petrol and diesel models. Not that electricity was particularly cheap. The UK still depended largely on gas for electricity generation, and the wholesale price of gas also shot up.

Those countries that already generated most of their electricity from renewables or nuclear were of course largely immune to these hikes in electricity price. France, producing 78 per cent of its electricity from nuclear and 10 per cent from renewables, emerged relatively unscathed; Norway, with 99 per cent hydroelectric power, did even better.

Why did this energy crunch happen? It was a combination of factors – growing demand in China and India, a reduction in supplies from the Middle East in the wake of the political instability that had followed the death of King Abdullah, and the failure of Russia to increase its production of oil and gas.

The energy crunch was enough to throw most of Europe and the United States into recession. The pattern of world trade was disrupted; Europe and America could no longer afford to import from China and the emerging Asian economies, which in any case were now focusing production on meeting the needs of a growing middle-class market at home. The overall effect was a substantial drop in living standards for most Europeans and North Americans. Food and clothing became substantially more expensive than they had been ten years earlier.

The big hike in energy costs drew some attention away from the issue of climate change. Governments continued to set individual national targets for CO_2 emissions: the UK, for example, stuck to its target of a 34 per cent reduction in CO_2 emissions by 2020 (compared with a 1990 baseline). However, despite the economic slowdown associated with the austerity in the early part of the decade, the reduction in transport-related CO_2 emissions as a result of the energy crunch and steady progress in replacement of coal- and gas-fired power stations with renewables and nuclear, the UK missed its 2020 CO_2 emissions targets. More significantly, the rest of the world, including China and the USA – the planet's largest emitters of CO_2 – continued to increase their emissions of greenhouse gases throughout this period. As a result, the world continues to get warmer.

Throughout the 2010s there were more extreme weather events throughout the world. There were unusually hot summers in 2014 and 2017, and severe flooding in the North of England in 2018.

2020 Onwards

Throughout the 2020s and 2030s, Western economies did a reasonably good job of recovering from the energy crunch, and gradually rebuilt themselves along low-carbon lines. Growth in China slowed somewhat, though it still exceeded that of most European countries. The big issue for the 2020s and 2030s was not energy, but global warming.

By 2040, the world had become 2°C warmer. Large parts of the world were facing drought and reduced crop yields. In Africa, around half a billion people were short of water and agricultural yields fell by 50 per cent, leading to starvation on a massive scale. In Asia, a billion people faced drought. Rice yields fell by 12 per cent in China, and maize and wheat yields by 5 per cent in India. In South America there were similar problems with drought and lower crop yields. Much tropical forest had returned to grassland, reducing the Earth's natural absorption of CO_2.

North America generally did well, as the northern states became warm enough for winter wheat, and overall yields increased by 20 per cent. Northern Europe and much of Russia similarly benefited, with an increase in production of wheat, soybeans and some fruit and vegetables. Southern Europe and the southern states of the USA, however, faced severe water shortages, and there would have been huge population transfers northwards had most states not closed their borders – the days of free trade and migration within the European Union were long gone.

As climate change disrupted patterns of agriculture everywhere, most nation states became much more insular in their outlook, focusing their efforts on feeding their own people. The New North of Scandinavian, Russian and Canadian states emerged as a new political grouping, with easy access to new oil reserves under the melting Arctic and a more beneficial climate for agriculture. Countries near the equator, especially in Africa and Asia, suffered terribly as sea levels rose and crops failed. All in all, the UK did quite well. Being an island with its own nuclear deterrent certainly helped: once Britons got used to the new economic order, they knuckled down quite well to producing most of their own food and goods, as they had done centuries before.

In Britain, summers became drier and warmer. By the 2050s, most places in the UK were experiencing average summer temperatures 2°C warmer than the 2020s. Because they accumulate heat, cities were warmer still. London was 3°C warmer in the 2050s, making its summer climate comparable to Southern France in the 2020s. Summer rainfall was down by 20 per cent or so, making water conservation an urgent issue for London and other towns and cities in the South of England.

British winters became milder, but wetter. In the northern uplands of Britain (roughly to the north and west of a line from the Severn estuary to the mouth of the Humber) average winter precipitation increased by 20 per cent.

In the southern lowlands of Britain rainfall was up by 25 per cent in the winter, and this went some way towards compensating for the summer drought.

Even as the world was getting used to a 2°C hike in temperature, the thermometer continued to rise. By 2075 the average temperature rise was 4°C. The picture then was much grimmer. Any potential increases in the agricultural productivity of North America, Northern Europe and Russia had been wiped out by further temperature rises. As a result, international trade in grain collapsed, and people in countries that could not feed themselves starved.

China faced enormous difficulties. With Himalayan glaciers pretty much all melted by 2070, there was no water to irrigate thirsty wheat and rice fields, and the country lacked the resources to feed its people. The links that China developed with Africa in the early part of the century didn't help, as Africa itself was more badly hit by climate change than any other continent. Tension between Russia and China increased as Chinese refugees attempted to move northwards into more temperate, just about self-sufficient, Russia.

By the end of the century, rising sea levels had had a dramatic effect on the world's geography, with average rises of just over 1 metre. During the course of the century almost 10 per cent of the world's population had relocated as homes and cities were flooded: Bombay, Los Angeles, Bangkok, Sydney and Amsterdam had disappeared entirely; Manhattan and Central London were also no longer inhabitable. Even in the comparatively hilly UK, a swathe of countryside from Cambridge to York disappeared below water, taking with it some of the country's most productive agricultural land.

HOW PLAUSIBLE IS THIS SCENARIO?

Many experts predict that some kind of energy crunch may well happen within the next ten years or so. The biggest single customer for oil in the world is the US military, which gets through about 100 million barrels of the stuff each year. It has a keen interest in trying to fathom out what's happening to the world's energy supplies, and this is what it said in a 2010 Joint Operating Environment report:

> By 2012, surplus oil production capacity could entirely disappear, and as early as 2015, the shortfall in output could reach nearly 10 million barrels per day. While it is difficult to predict precisely what economic, political, and strategic effects such a shortfall might produce, it surely

would reduce the prospects for growth in both the developing and developed worlds. Such an economic slowdown would exacerbate other unresolved tensions, push fragile and failing states further down the path toward collapse, and perhaps have serious economic impact on both China and India.

It's not alone. The UK Task Force on Peak Oil and Energy Security predicts a similar energy crunch, which could come as soon as 2013.

Not everyone agrees that there will be an energy crunch of this kind. Many in the oil industry assume that better technology will enable more oil to be recovered from existing and unconventional wells. They predict that oil and gas supplies will continue to rise for a decade or more, until they reach some kind of plateau. Supplies could remain at this high level for a number of years, allowing for new energy sources – renewables and nuclear – to ramp up to meet increasing demand. Even if supplies of oil and gas prove difficult, by most estimates the world still has plenty of coal to burn for electricity.

Plentiful fossil fuels may postpone the energy crunch indefinitely, but burning them will make climate change significantly worse.

I've based this scenario on data from the UK's Meteorological Office. According to a 2008 report, if greenhouse gas emissions continue to rise at present rates, then the most likely outcome is a 5.5 per cent rise in global temperatures by the end of the twenty-first century. This translates into a 2°C rise around 2040, and a 4°C rise in the 2070s.

The trend towards hotter, drier summers and milder, wetter winters is already happening, but that doesn't mean that we won't also experience weather events that superficially appear to contradict the general pattern, such as the exceptionally cold and snowy winters of 2009 and 2010.

The last decade has seen an unusually large number of extreme weather events in the UK: the hot summer of 2003, floods in Boscastle in 2004, Sheffield in 2007 and Cumbria in 2009. The frequency and impact of extreme weather events is likely to increase.

Remember that this is a scenario, not a prediction. I'm not predicting an energy crunch in 2016. It may happen any time in the next ten years, or not at all. While it seems highly likely that the world will pass the 2°C tipping point some time in this century, no one knows precisely when that will be. The point of scenario planning is to be prepared for such events if they do come to pass.

WHAT DOES THIS MEAN FOR YOUR BUSINESS?

This scenario is far from certain – it may not even be likely, but it's surely possible. If you knew that something like this was on the horizon, what would your business need to do in order to prepare for it?

At the top of the list would be to make your business more energy-efficient. The more quickly energy prices rise, the more competitive advantage your business will have if its energy usage is low.

If your business is dependent on global trade, with customers, suppliers or both, you might want to consider the effects of a slowdown on cheap and easy global commerce.

And finally, if climate change will continue to mean more extreme weather events, you might want to think about any mitigation measures to minimise the effects of extreme weather on your business.

8

Conflict

Market forces may be great most of the time, but when it comes to genuine resource scarcity, governments always step in. They rig markets, they seize resources and, all too often, they go to war.
        Stephen King, Managing Director of Economics at HSBC

We are all addicts of fossil fuels in a state of denial, about to face cold turkey. And like so many addicts about to face cold turkey, our leaders are now committing violent crimes to get what little is left of what we're hooked on.
        Kurt Vonnegut, author

Until 2020

The early years of the 2010s were dominated by conflict within countries. Rising world food and energy prices had driven up the cost of everyday living in many parts of the world, and what had been isolated and uncoordinated food riots during the early years of the century coalesced into highly co-ordinated attempts to overthrow repressive governments, particularly in the Arab world. Popular uprisings in Tunisia and Egypt which had led to the rapid overthrow of long-established dictators encouraged people throughout the Arab world to rise up against dictatorial governments. These movements were most successful in relatively poor countries like Yemen and Sudan. The governments of oil-rich countries like Libya and Iran found it much easier to repress popular dissent with their customary brutality – at least while the oil revenues continued to flow. Even this strategy was not always successful, as the overthrow of Libyan dictator Gaddafi demonstrated in 2011.

Internationally, tensions remained high, especially between Russia and Europe. This dispute crystallised around the question of access to the Arctic and its estimated 90 billion barrels of oil – enough to keep the world going at

2010 rates of consumption for another three years. All parties agreed with the longstanding convention that mineral rights extend 350 nautical miles off their coastline, providing their continental shelf extends that far. According to the Russians, an underwater ridge called the Lomonosov Ridge was part of the Russian Continental Shelf, and they therefore claimed all the mineral rights up to the North Pole itself. In 2012 Russia began drilling, while both Norway and Denmark claimed those parts of the Arctic as their own. Although it never came to a shooting match, tensions were very high, and Russia restricted its sales of oil and gas to all European countries, turning to China instead as its main customer. The Nordstream gas pipeline, which at one point had supplied more than 26 million EU households with gas, was finally turned off completely in 2016. This further drove up energy prices throughout Europe. A new Cold War seemed to be developing between the Europeans and Russia. The added complication was that the world's biggest economy, China, now appeared to be allied with Russia.

The critical event which precipitated the 2018 energy crisis happened not in the Middle East, nor in Russia, but in the Straits of Malacca, a 500-mile-long waterway between Malaysia and Indonesia. In February 2018 terrorists hijacked an oil tanker and detonated a nuclear bomb on board, close to the narrowest point of the Straits. At the time half of China's total imports and two-thirds of the world's internationally traded liquid petroleum gas was passing along the waterway. Although some of this was immediately rerouted south of Sumatra, the 2,000-mile detour had an immediate effect on energy prices, causing the price of oil and gas to double overnight.

Rising energy prices caused a great deal of unease in the developed world, and this 2018 energy crunch led to many changes of government throughout Europe, although these were all achieved through the formal democratic process. Incoming governments had some tough choices to make. Having been elected on the promise of reducing energy costs, the only way to achieve that in the short term was to reduce energy taxes. This hit government revenues very hard, creating a vicious cycle in which further cuts in public services were required to balance the books.

2020 Onwards

Although by 2020 the faltering world economy was reducing the demand for oil, the supply of oil was declining faster still – partly as a result of the slowdown in physical production from the Middle East as mature oilfields went into decline, partly because political factors prevented new oil from Russia coming onto the market, and partly because of distribution problems associated with the events in the Malacca Straits. By 2023 oil finally hit its all-time record price of $300 a barrel, and it was clear to everyone that never again would the world enjoy cheap fossil fuel energy.

Even the oil-rich Middle Eastern states were now finding it hard to control their populations – although the price of oil was high, supplies were dwindling. With little agriculture or manufacture, and unable to afford the huge imports of grain to feed their populations, many formerly oil-rich states were in meltdown. Internal instability finally blew up into full-scale war when Iran and Israel unleashed nuclear weapons against each other in 2024. China, the USA, Russia and Europe were too busy trying to manage their own economies to care much.

By 2030 the population of China was peaking at around 1.5 billion and its agriculture was in trouble. Some parts of China had already warmed more than 3°C above pre-industrial levels. In the northern plain, where most of the wheat was grown, production in 2032 was 60 per cent down on levels of ten years earlier. As a result, China became dependent on Russia not only for energy, but also for food, and this relationship was not an easy one. Tensions between the two superpowers grew as China became increasingly frustrated at the high cost of Russian food and energy, and began to look enviously at the sparsely populated, resource-rich Siberia and Russian Far Eastern territories.

As global warming began to make its full effects felt on world food production, individual nation states increasingly turned inwards, trading with relatively few trusted partners only as much as was necessary. The biggest global conflict of the century was still to come, and it was not about oil, but water.

Both India and Pakistan had always relied heavily on water from the six rivers of the Indus system that rises high in the Himalayas. Who got what from the Indus had always been a bone of contention between India and Pakistan since the original British colony had been partitioned into two independent states in 1948. The issue had been kept under the lid by a treaty in 1960 which allocated three rivers' waters to India and three to Pakistan.

By mid-century Pakistan's three rivers, largely dependent on glacial melt, had all but stopped flowing, destroying the prospects of growing any crops on the three-quarters of Pakistan's land mass they irrigated. Meanwhile, the three Indian rivers were still flowing, as they depend more on rainfall than glacier melt. With both India and Pakistan's long history of enmity, and nuclear weapons on both sides, demands from a new radical government in Pakistan soon led to guerrilla actions on Indian water supplies. This in turn provoked reprisals by the Indian government and a limited use of nuclear weapons. This soon escalated into widespread use of nuclear weapons on both sides. Eventually, 500 million people died, a third of the two countries' combined population.

HOW PLAUSIBLE IS THIS SCENARIO?

Competition for resources has always been a key component of conflict. William the Conqueror's attack on Saxon Britain in 1066 may have been driven by pride and ambition, but he timed the invasion for the autumn to be sure that the harvest had been gathered in first. Hitler had a vision of a Reich that would last a thousand years, but it was Polish coal and Russian oil that made those countries especially attractive targets for conquest. And as former Federal Reserve chairman Alan Greenspan wryly admitted, the 2003 invasion of Iraq by the United States was largely about oil.

I'm unlikely to be right about the specifics of terrorist disruption to world trade in the Malacca Straits, tensions between Russia and Europe, or an Israel–Iran war, and I certainly hope to be entirely wrong about nuclear conflict between India and Pakistan, but if these political flashpoints don't erupt into bitter and bloody conflicts, others almost certainly will.

Political upheavals in the Middle East are already happening in 2012, and Russia had already staked a claim to Arctic oil in 2007 by the time Vladimir Putin's friend Artur Chilingarov took a submarine under the North Pole and planted a Russian flag on the seabed.

Terrorists and other violent groups already have a major impact on energy supply and price, as energy expert Daniel Yergin points out in his book *The Quest: Energy, Security and the Remaking of the Modern World*. Kidnapping, intimidation and oil theft by independent militias in Nigeria in the years leading up to 2009 resulted in losses of up to a million barrels a day from Nigeria's oil exports, and were a significant contributory factor to the $147 a barrel oil price spike of that year. The most critical choke point for oil supplies is the Strait of Hormuz, though which a quarter of the world's oil production travels on its way out of the Persian Gulf. Disruption of this sea lane has long been at the top of terrorist wish lists, but the area is reasonably well patrolled by the US Navy, so in my scenario I have chosen the more vulnerable Straits of Malacca.

By 2050, Russia will have a population of around 140 million and could be doing relatively well as a country: it has substantial reserves of oil, gas and coal, and climate change will probably increase the productivity of its wheat harvests. China, by contrast, with 1.5 billion people, will not only be running short of fossil fuels, but will be struggling to feed its population as climate change decimates crops of rice in the south of the country and wheat in the north. If China decided that it wanted its share of the world's resources from its northern neighbour, the consequences could be dramatic.

While it's clear that scarce resources have always led to conflict between nations, it's also true that abundant resources ultimately lead to conflict within nations. Here's why.

When a country discovers abundant oil and gas resources, three bad things tend to happen. The first is known as 'the Dutch disease', because this is what happened to Holland when it began exporting gas in the 1960s. As revenues from oil and gas begin to flow into a country, the national currency becomes overvalued and exports become more expensive. Local businesses struggle, partly because they can no longer compete against cheap imports, and partly because government sees no need to encourage local firms when the nation's coffers are full of oil and gas money.

This leads to the second difficulty, the so-called 'reverse Midas touch'. Oil and gas generate a lot of money, but relatively few jobs. As other businesses decline, governments are forced to subsidise food, fuel and unproductive jobs simply to maintain a stable society. This is fine when those oil and gas revenues flow, but highly problematic should they decline for any reason.

This in turn leads to a third difficulty, often known as 'the resource curse'. As oil and gas revenues increase, corruption tends to grow and democracy tends to decline. With few exceptions, as Tom Friedman points out in *Hot, Flat and Crowded*, there is an almost perfect negative correlation between oil price and democracy.

Saudi Arabia, the world's biggest oil and gas exporter with 90 per cent of its exports based on the $900 million of oil it sells every day, is an absolute monarchy where women are not allowed to drive or vote. Russia, the number two exporter of oil and gas, may have regular elections, but the real power is held by Vladimir Putin and his close associates.

There are some exceptions to the rule. Norway has benefited from considerable exports of its North Sea oil and gas since the 1970s, and has seen no reduction in democracy or freedom of speech. It has used oil and gas revenues primarily to pay off its foreign debt and establish a sovereign wealth fund now worth about $750 billion. In 2012, while most European countries were struggling with austerity measures to tackle increasing national debts, Norway was able to look on with some complacency.

While the specifics of my conflict scenario are unlikely to come to pass, the general idea that competition for resources will lead to conflict within and between nation states is uncontroversial. Historically, as Jared Diamond explains in his book *Collapse*, civilised societies have often collapsed when they've exhausted the natural resources that made them great in the first place: some people think that such a collapse might be what's in prospect for us. Environmentalist James Lovelock, for example, has written that he expects the world population at the end of this century to be only 20 per cent of what it is now.

While most experts consider the complete collapse of civilisation unlikely, there's widespread agreement that dwindling resources leads to more conflict. If this does happen, what are the consequences for you and your business?

WHAT DOES THIS MEAN FOR YOUR BUSINESS?

If energy resources are scarce, you can protect your business not only by becoming more energy-efficient, but also by becoming less energy-dependent. As electricity generation moves from a small number of large power stations to a very large number of small sources of power, generating your own power becomes both desirable and feasible for many businesses.

If global or regional conflict affects some of your trading partners, how can you minimise the risks of disruption to your business?

If your company wishes to be seen as an ethical business, you might want to consider the fact that your use of fossil fuels continues to maintain undemocratic regimes in many parts of the world, including the Middle East, Russia and parts of Africa and South America.

9

Technology to the Rescue

All it takes to improve living standards is to make sure energy is cheap and let people work for each other through trade, to let ideas meet and mate – and innovation follows. Good as life is compared with the past, the future is going to be much better.

Matt Ridley, *author of* The Rational Optimist

Until 2020

The energy crunch predicted by many to occur some time between 2010 and 2020 never came. While the price of energy remained high – oil was consistently traded at $120–200 a barrel throughout this decade – supplies never dried up, despite rapidly increasing demand.

The reason for this was simple – better technology. In some cases this meant incremental improvements in existing technologies. When the Queen pushed a gold-plated button in BP's Aberdeen headquarters in 1975 to begin the flow of oil from the UK's North Sea Forties field, no one expected the flow to continue much beyond 2010. With better methods of accessing the oil, the Forties still produces 16,000 barrels a day in 2012, and is likely to still be pumping in 2027.

In other cases, technology that was once peripheral became mainstream. In the first part of the new century, extracting gas from shale rocks through 'fracking' – pumping a high-pressure mixture of water and chemicals into porous rock to force out the gas – was highly controversial. Its critics accused it of poisoning groundwater supplies and even causing earthquakes. In 2000 shale gas accounted for just 1 per cent of the USA's natural gas supplies. By 2011 shale gas had transformed the US energy market and accounted for 25 per cent of all natural gas supplies. By 2020 it was 40 per cent.

Although shale gas was never a big hit in Europe during this period, the huge increase in the US market had knock-on effects throughout the world, effectively keeping the price lower than it would otherwise have been. It also helped with greenhouse gas emissions – electricity from gas produces a third of the emissions as electricity from conventional coal-fired power stations.

Shale gas also created a bit of breathing space for the development of non-fossil fuel energy technologies. The big success story of the decade leading up to 2020 was solar power. As far back as 2011 solar photovoltaic was supplying power in California at a lower price than gas-fired power stations. Breakthroughs in the cost and efficiency of solar PV made solar power cheaper in many countries than fossil fuel electricity from the grid, and the technology spread rapidly. However, solar's biggest contribution wasn't PV, but concentrated solar power (CSP). In 2015 Desertec opened its first concentrated solar power station in Morocco, supplying 1GW of power to the European grid though high-voltage DC lines. A further 5GW of capacity was added by the end of the decade.

Almost as significant at this time were the significant advances in battery power. When mainstream electric vehicles (EVs) first took to the roads in 2012, the phrase on every driver's lips was 'range anxiety'. Early EVs had a range of only about 100 miles, and took hours to recharge. By 2020 batteries were lighter, cheaper, more powerful and quicker to recharge. The typical EV now had a 400-mile range and could be recharged in less than 20 minutes.

2020 Onwards

The other surprising development was nuclear. Early in the decade many governments had followed France's lead and commissioned a few large-scale nuclear power stations, each generating about 1GW of power. By the time these were built and online, the whole way of thinking about electricity had changed. In 2010 the model had been a few large power stations delivering constantly priced electricity one-way to dumb devices. By 2020 the model was changing rapidly to the form it would finally assume in most countries by 2030: a huge number of very small generators delivering power at constantly changing prices to smart devices. This led to some surprising developments, one of which was small-scale nuclear. In the period 2020–30 very few large-scale nuclear power stations were built, but thousands of small-scale nuclear plants in the 30–300MW range were assembled in factories, to be used either for small-scale electricity generation or as power plants for large ships.

Another surprising consequence of the smart grid approach to electricity was that by 2030 the average European EV driver essentially drove for free. The cost of charging the car at night, when electricity was very cheap, was more than offset by selling some of the power in the car's batteries during the daytime when electricity cost much more. A typical night's charge provided enough power for 400 miles of motoring, but with the average European daily commute being only 15 miles, there was plenty of scope for selling the power back to the grid in the daytime at a higher price. By 2030 more than half of Europe's 300 million cars were electric.

While renewable energy continued to develop throughout the 2030s and beyond, the most significant technological advances in the period 2030–50 were in food and agriculture. A widespread acceptance of genetically modified (GM) food led to the development of crops which gave bigger yields, required less water, and were generally much more resistant to extreme changes in temperature that had been so detrimental to traditional crops. GM crops went a long way to tackling two of the major challenges the world was facing in 2050 – how to feed a greatly increased world population of 9 million people when traditional crops were yielding less as a result of climate change.

A completely new approach to food was required to deal with the increasing desire for meat in China, India and the world's newest developed economies. In 2011 the world's first in vitro meat – meat grown in a laboratory from a few animal cells – was a mere curiosity. By 2030 it was a mainstream industry, and by 2050 it was feeding more people than traditional farm-grown animals.

Despite a big move towards renewable energy in the early part of the century, the world continued to get warmer. Some of the world's largest economies, including China and the USA, continued to burn coal for much of the 2010s, and techniques of carbon capture and storage were never cheap enough to be economically viable. Despite many European countries hitting their CO_2 reduction targets by 2020, the world's carbon emissions overall continued to rise until 2025, and only then began to stabilise and decrease. As a result, temperatures continued to rise and the psychologically important tipping point of 2°C was expected in 2070. Thanks to new technology, the world's population of 9 billion people was coping relatively well. Nevertheless, there was widespread acceptance that further temperature rise was both likely and undesirable.

The big issue of the 2030s was the debate over geo-engineering. Should the power of science be used to cool the world directly, perhaps by blocking out a proportion of the Sun's rays in some way? The debate was long and vigorous, with most European countries arguing that it was dangerous to meddle with the world ecology in such a way. Further limitations on greenhouse gases and a strong focus on adaptation to climate change was the way forward. China, India and Russia, however, argued that it was too late for all that – there was already sufficient CO_2 in the atmosphere to cause unacceptable levels of warming for generations to come unless decisive action was taken quickly.

Despite various attempts at international agreement, no consensus had been reached by 2038. In that year the Chinese government launched a fleet of 80 specially designed aircraft to release sulphur aerosols into the atmosphere. By absorbing sunlight, the sulphur particulates had the desired effect of cooling the Earth's atmosphere. Despite some unpleasant side effects such as acid rain, the programme achieved its outcome of stabilising the world's temperature. With an annual cost of 6 billion yuan (about US$1 billion), the Chinese government was happy to save the world at a cost of less than US$1 per head of its population. As China was now the world's undisputed economic and military power, no other nation made much of a protest. Most of the governments that had argued against geo-engineering were secretly rather relieved that it had all turned out so well.

HOW PLAUSIBLE IS THIS SCENARIO?

In 1798 a grumpy Victorian clergyman called Thomas Malthus famously predicted that mass starvation lay ahead for much of the world's population since the increase in land available for food production could never keep up with the rise in population. And yet in 2012, with a world population of 7 billion people, fewer people starve than in Malthus's day, when only 1 billion people lived on the planet. How come?

In a word: technology. Even in Malthus's day agricultural yields were improving thanks to nitrogen fertiliser in the shape of guano, largely harvested from small islands off the coast of Africa and South America, where the accumulated droppings of cormorants, boobies, penguins and other birds had deposited thick layers of bird shit over hundreds of years. Just as the guano was starting to run out in the early twentieth century, along came two boffins called Fritz Haber and Carl Bosch, who discovered a way of producing nitrogen fertiliser from steam, methane and air. It is this process that's used to produce almost all the nitrogen-based fertiliser which makes farms so productive today. Other technologies have continued to help along the way, most notably the green revolution of the 1960s, with better fertilisers, pesticides and higher-yielding strains of crop. A series of small improvements in agriculture, including no-till techniques, means that the same amount of land now feeds twice as many people in 2012 as it did in 1960. This is just as well, as the world's population has more than doubled in that time too. So although I may be wrong about GM foods and in vitro meat, the 9 million inhabitants of the world in 2050 will need some kind of technological fix to feed them, because there simply isn't enough land with conventional methods.

While we're likely to see a big increase in renewable energy, no one knows which technologies will be the winners. In this scenario, I've plumped for solar, batteries and small-scale nuclear, but I might be completely wrong – wind power, biofuels from algae and really big nuclear power might be the technological fixes we come to depend on.

My final observations in this scenario are on geo-engineering. Without drastic action, the chances of keeping climate change to a rise of less than 2°C are pretty small. Even if all greenhouse gas emissions stopped immediately, there's enough CO_2 already there to mean we have a more than even chance of hitting 2°C sometime this century. Every extra tonne of CO_2 – and in 2012 we're adding about 1,000 tonnes of CO_2 every second – makes that 2°C rise more likely to happen, and more likely to happen sooner. If you can't mitigate climate change by reducing emissions quickly enough, and if you can't adapt to it because the effects are too severe, the only option you have left is geo-engineering: meddling with the Earth's systems on a large scale to halt or reverse global warming.

There are two main approaches to geo-engineering. Air capture (AC) means taking CO_2 out of the atmosphere and storing it safely somewhere, or even converting it into something useful. One way is to sprinkle nitrogen, iron or phosphates onto the ocean in order to promote the growth of naturally occurring marine algae that absorb CO_2, and then fall to the bottom of the ocean bed, where the CO_2 remains, to all intents and purposes, for ever. Another approach is to build a kind of artificial tree, a machine which grabs CO_2 from the atmosphere and then stores it underground. Neither of these approaches turned out to be that promising. In 2007 Richard Branson put up a $25 million prize for anyone who could come up with a practical method for removing 1 billion tonnes of carbon per year from the atmosphere, but it remains unclaimed.

The rival to air capture is solar radiation management (SRM). Don't worry about how much CO_2 gets into the air – cool the planet by reducing the amount of sunlight hitting the Earth.

Some SRM technologies have been a bit mad. One proposal, for example, was to put thousands of small sunshades in orbit around the Sun, at the exact point where they would cast a shadow onto the Earth, thus reducing the amount of sunlight hitting the Earth. Could it have worked? We'll never know, because the cost was enough to prevent it ever being tested.

Two SRM technologies appear more promising. The first is marine cloud whitening. Two British scientists, John Latham and Stephen Salter, had researched the idea that if you spray a very fine mist of water droplets into the air from the top of a ship, these droplets would rise to the level of the marine cloud layer and produce more, whiter clouds. More, whiter clouds means less sunlight reaching the Earth and less global warming. In 2010, Bill Gates's Microsoft Foundation funded some small experiments to increase the reflectivity of clouds by spraying salt water into the air, but the trials were unpopular with both environmental groups and the general public, and the results were inconclusive.

The second approach is to use sulphur aerosols. In 2006 a scientist called Paul Crutzen observed that after a volcano called Mount Pinatubo had erupted in 1991, spewing 15 billion tonnes of sulphur dioxide into the air, the average global temperature dropped for two successive years and didn't resume an upward trend once more until 1993. The cloud of sulphate aerosols had covered the entire planet, blocked out some of the Sun's energy and caused two years of global cooling. Why not mimic the Pinatubo effect by equipping a fleet of aircraft to spray sulphates directly into the atmosphere?

Geo-engineering in general, and solar radiation management in particular, is deeply controversial. The argument against is that it's dangerous to meddle with the Earth on such a large scale – who knows what might happen? The argument in favour is that we're already meddling with the Earth on a large scale by pumping vast quantities of greenhouse gases into the atmosphere, and we are fast running out of other options. Time will tell which argument wins the day.

WHAT DOES THIS MEAN FOR YOUR BUSINESS?

In comparison with my two previous scenarios – 'Present Trends Continue' and 'Conflict', 'Technology to the Rescue' is a much more optimistic view of the future. But like the other two, it's a scenario, not a prediction. We can hope that technological advances will enable most of the 9 billion people in 2050 and beyond to live a reasonable tolerable lifestyle, but we don't know what those technologies will be. Look at any 1950s science fiction movie: the advances they predicted – robots doing all the work, instant nutrition from pills, holidays on the Moon – turned out to be precisely wrong, while the technology that really makes a difference – smartphones, the Internet – barely got a look-in.

We can be certain that new technologies will be developed that will have a huge impact on the quality of our lives, we just can't predict what they will be. Successful businesses will continue to be agile and adaptable, so that they can adopt those technologies that turn out to be significant, and drop those which turn out to be irrelevant.

10

Less is More

Infinite high resource intensity growth is simply not possible, and we are already living off our future capital. It may be gradual, but most businesses will have to adjust to a very different reality. That reality will still be a version of capitalism, and needs to be a positive vision rather than a doom-laden return to the Stone Age, but it needs to rethink the point of the system. Instead of the goal of maximum linear growth in GDP, we should be thinking of maximum wellbeing for minimal planetary input.

Ian Cartwright, CEO, Kingfisher

Until 2020

The period 2010–2020 became known as the decade of austerity. This was particularly true for Europe, the USA and Japan. The knock-on effects of the 2008–2009 banking crisis were particularly severe in Europe. The effects were worse in Ireland, Greece and Portugal, all of which eventually defaulted on their debts, but every European country experienced rises in taxation, and reductions in public expenditure and individual disposable income. It took Japan the whole of this decade to recover fully from the 2011 tsunami, while the US economy seemed permanently stalled. Although growth continued in China, India, Brazil, and to some extent Russia, it was at a considerably lower rate than the previous ten years. Energy prices were highly volatile throughout the decade, but the trend was clearly upwards, and by 2020 oil was trading at more than $200 a barrel. Rising energy costs and rising world population led to a doubling in the price of most foodstuffs between 2010 and 2020.

In the UK, most Britons found themselves adapting surprisingly well to their more straitened circumstances. With fuel at record prices, people drove less. Those still in jobs found that their employers were increasingly encouraging them to work from home for at least part of the working week, and this trend accelerated rapidly throughout the decade. Even those people who still went out to work began to look for jobs more locally. As people began spending a higher proportion of their time in or near to where they lived, there was a resurgence of what another era had called civic pride – people felt much more connected to their local communities, whether in villages, towns or cities.

With soaring energy prices, high levels of energy efficiency became commonplace in almost every building. By the end of the decade, all new housing was effectively carbon-neutral, being built to high levels of insulation with local sources of power and heat. Since low-carbon building commanded a premium price, there was no longer any incentive to build in any other way. Thanks to the UK government's Green Deal, which turned out to be much more successful than anybody had anticipated, the vast majority of the UK's housing stock was retrofitted with insulation and more efficient heating and lighting systems by 2020.

People became much more frugal, not only in their use of energy, but in their use of almost everything. People discovered that they could make their clothes, TVs, computers, and household gadgets last a lot longer before they replaced or upgraded them. There was less waste of food – in 2010, 20 per cent of all food bought in the UK was thrown away, and this figure declined sharply as food prices continued to rise. The big out-of-town shopping centres found their trade declining, and more people shopped locally. The Co-operative's chain of locally based foodstores continued to gain market share, and by 2020 it had overtaken some of its rivals to be the second largest supermarket chain. While most food continued to be purchased, increasing numbers of people grew some of their own food.

One of the biggest successes of the decade was the transition towns movement, a grassroots effort to create communities that could thrive even as energy prices skyrocketed. This often involved more frugal use of energy, local energy generation, local food production and a resurgence of local craft skills. Some even adopted a local currency. The earliest transition towns, such as Totnes in Devon, had a reputation for being slightly eccentric, but as national economies stalled in 2010–2020, the idea became more mainstream. At the beginning of this decade, fossil fuel energy was still cheaper than renewable energy. By the end of the decade, the situation was reversed. It no longer made sense for national governments to run huge fossil fuel power stations where half of the energy disappeared in wasted heat up a cooling tower before it could be fed into the national grid. As coal, nuclear and eventually gas-fired power stations were gradually phased out, they were replaced by small to medium-sized power generation facilities, many of which were owned by municipal authorities. As people became much more frugal in their use of energy, overall demand decreased, despite the fact that both transport and heating were eventually mainly powered by electricity in the form of electric vehicles and heat pumps respectively. This meant that a wide variety of power supply was able to meet demand, and although there was still a national grid for electricity, people tended to look towards their local source of supply. It made much more sense for local communities to develop their own local sources of renewable power, whether that was a small-scale hydroelectric plant serving a small village or an offshore windfarm supplying the needs of a large town.

More generally, as national governments offered less to their citizens while they continued to struggle with large debts and dwindling tax receipts, people increasingly looked to their local communities to meet their needs.

The biggest change of all during this period was not economic, but psychological. Most people discovered, somewhat to their surprise, that they rather liked living more frugally. People started to take pride in making things last longer, and looked back on the rampant consumerism of the late twentieth century with distaste. The most successful businesses were those that produced sensible, long-lasting products, in a sustainable way.

While much of Europe and the developed world experienced similar shifts in habits and attitudes to the UK, the picture in the developing world, where most people had never had very much in the way of consumer goods, was very different. China, India and other developing economies continued to grow throughout this decade, although the rate of growth decreased each year. As wages rose within these countries, their economies moved away from ultra-low-cost exports and towards more moderately priced goods and services for the growing domestic middle class.

By 2020, more than 60 per cent of the world's population were city dwellers – a big increase since 2008, when the number of global urban dwellers exceeded 50 per cent for the first time. The reasons for the continuing growth in cities were not hard to see: they are the most effective social structures for innovation, economic growth and improving living standards, offering a better quality of life for many people than the reality of grinding rural poverty. They are also an extremely energy- and resource-efficient way of living. It requires a lot more energy to transport yourself from one village to another by car or bus than it does to use mass transit in a city – and even less to walk or cycle. Economies of scale and lower transmission costs mean that electricity and heating are more efficient in a city too. Although it was playing out in a different way, it seemed that in the developing world, as well as in the developed world, the focus was on the local community rather than the national one.

Towards 2050

The world's population continued to grow throughout the 2020s, 2030s and 2040s, eventually levelling out at around 9 billion in 2015. This had two consequences: one predictable, one surprising.

The predictable consequence was huge demand for finite resources. Fossil fuels, water, agricultural land, metals and minerals are all finite resources. When the Industrial Revolution really got going around the beginning of the nineteenth century, and the world's population was just 1 billion, it must have seemed that these resources would last forever. But when the world's population reached 8 billion in 2027, it was clear that they wouldn't. Despite technological advances in energy and agriculture, by 2030 or so there was a general acceptance that we could no longer afford to be profligate with the world's resources.

As food prices continued to rise, more people began to eat locally grown food, and many countries produced more of their own food. Self-sufficiency in food, the twentieth-century environmentalist's dream, was never feasible at the level of individuals or families. It's just about possible to grow enough food to live on in the UK if you have an acre or two of land, but it's extremely hard work. Back in the eighteenth century, economist David Ricardo had shown that you'll enjoy a better standard of living if you do what you're good at and trade with others for the things you want: he called it the law of comparative advantage. This philosophy had driven globalisation throughout the twentieth century and made a lot of people a lot better off, at least materially. While transport costs were low, it did indeed make sense to buy food from all over the world. But as energy costs, and therefore transport costs, increased in the twenty-first century, the global trade in food began to decline. By 2030 it made sense to source more food locally, and during this decade most countries had as a matter of policy become more self-sufficient in food.

Not only did the overall population increase, so did the proportion of older people almost everywhere. By 2050, most European countries had three older dependents for every four people of working age. It was probably this demographic shift which led to the most surprising consequence of population growth: a rejection of consumerism. In the developed world it became deeply unfashionable to flaunt material goods. As stuff became less important in people's lives, the gap between rich and poor, which had been steadily increasing in many developed nations during the late twentieth and early twenty-first centuries, began to reduce once more. As societies became more equal, people at all levels in those societies found themselves becoming more content with life.

The nature of business changed too. Even in the early years of the twenty-first century, the pursuit of profit had been the primary driver for most businesses. By 2030, a new generation of business leaders saw things a little differently. Improving the quality of people's lives became a bigger driver than simple profit. In an era of frugality, many former products became services, to be rented by the hour rather than bought outright. By 2030, very few people bought cars, domestic appliances or computers; most rented them as a service. It made no sense to buy an expensive electric car when you could easily rent one full-time or part-time, according to your needs.

The nature of the workplace changed. More people worked from home than travelled to an office or factory to work, and more people worked part-time than full-time. In the twentieth century, businesses became more efficient by getting fewer employees to do more work; in the twenty-first century, businesses became more efficient by getting the same number of people to work less. As the demographics shifted towards older people and the number of younger people entering the workplace diminished, firms competed fiercely for new talent – and both the experienced older workers and the energetic newer ones were generally attracted to the companies that offered the best work–life balance rather than the highest salary.

Perhaps most significantly of all, the nature of national economies changed. Even in the early years of the twenty-first century, economic growth, as measured by an increase in GDP, was deemed to be a good thing, while a lack of growth – recession – was to be avoided at all costs. What was strange about the middle years of the twenty-first century was that people seemed to be enjoying an ever-increasing quality of life, despite the lack of economic growth. During the 2030s, a handful of countries, including Denmark, Sweden and Japan, officially declared that their primary economic objective was prosperity without growth – meaning an increase in wellbeing with a zero increase in GDP, and the success of these countries led to similar economic objectives being adopted, sometimes explicitly, sometimes more covertly, in many nations by 2050.

HOW PLAUSIBLE IS THIS SCENARIO?

This scenario is based on two key assumptions: firstly, that increasing demand for finite resources will result in a more frugal lifestyle for everyone, and secondly, that it's possible to have a better quality of life with less stuff – the rejection of consumerism, if you will.

It seems self-evident that a single planet with finite resources can't support an increasing population for ever, at least not if that population expects an ever-increasing standard of material wealth. Our current economic model relies on natural resources – fossil fuels, water, wood, uranium, metals and minerals – and although these resources are very large, they are finite. The world economy has grown over the last 25 years or so at an average rate of around 3 per cent in real terms. At this rate, it will double in size every 23 years. It's hard to imagine that we'll be able to access twice as many primary resources in 2034 and four times as many in 2050, given that those resources are already scarce and expensive now.

Hard to imagine, but not impossible – after all, we've been here before. In 1968, Paul Ehrlich's best-selling book *The Population Bomb* predicted mass famine and the deaths of millions as population outstripped natural resources. The mass famines still haven't happened, even though the world's population is now twice what it is when Ehrlich wrote the book, for reasons we discussed in Chapter 9 – technology has enabled us to do more with less. In a famous bet, economist Julian Simon challenged Ehrlich in 1980 to choose five key natural resources. If the price (in real terms) went up during the next ten years, Ehrlich would win, but if the price went down, Simon would be the victor. By 1990, every single one of Ehrlich's chosen commodities – copper, chromium, nickel, tin and tungsten – had declined in price. A chagrined Paul Ehrlich handed over $576.07 to Simon.

But just because Ehrlich was wrong in practice, it doesn't mean he was wrong in principle: in fact, if Ehrlich had extended the challenge to 2012, he would have won the bet handsomely. It all depends on whether improved technology can reduce our resource-intensity faster than growing population and growing aspirations can increase it. Technology has won some battles, but lost others. The world's population has doubled since 1969, but so has the productivity of land, through a combination of better breeds of crops, cleverer farming methods and nitrogen-based fertiliser – a victory for technology. We haven't been so clever with oil. In 1969 we used 49mbpd, and in 2012, with twice the number of people, we're using almost twice as much oil – 88mbpd. There's been hardly any improvement in resource-intensity at all.

Is it possible to reject consumerism and enjoy a better quality of life? Or to put this another way: does money make you happy? Up to a point, according to economist Richard Layard. Research on happiness indicates that in countries with an average per capita income of less than $10,000, income and happiness are quite strongly correlated – the more you earn, the happier you are. It's difficult to be precise, as notions of happiness are probably quite strongly influenced by national culture. However, most researchers agree that above this basic level, increased material wealth doesn't contribute to increased happiness. In the UK, like most of western Europe, average disposable income more than doubled in the period 1950–2000. Levels of happiness, however, have remained constant or even slightly declined.

If money doesn't buy happiness, what does? Layard identifies seven key factors which contribute most to happiness – family relationships, financial situation, work, friends, health, personal freedom and personal values. The interesting thing about financial situation in this list is that it's not absolute levels of income that make the difference – it's comparison with others. People who earn £60,000 while their peer group earn £50,000 tend to be happier than those who earn £70,000 while their peers earn £80,000. In a separate study, Richard Wilkinson and Kate Pickett point out in their book *The Spirit Level* that more equal societies like Norway, Sweden and Japan tend to report higher levels of trust and happiness, as well as less obesity, better health and longer life expectancy than more unequal societies like Britain and the USA.

If consumerism doesn't make us happy, why is it that so many us seem devoted to economic gain, even if we know that it means less of the things that make us happy – family relationships, time with friends, personal freedom? Because we're hard-wired to do so. When human beings first evolved on the African savannah some 200,000 years ago, it made good sense to eat as much sugary, fatty food as we could – when food's scarce, it makes sense to eat as much as you can. But when food's abundant, as it is for many people living in the developed world of the early twenty-first century, consistently eating as much as you can makes no sense at all – it leads to obesity, heart disease and early death. But we're hard-wired to do so. Many of the quirks of human beings – our failure to plan properly for the long term, our irrational approach to risk (why does flying feel so much more dangerous than driving a car, when statistically the opposite is true?), our willingness to take key decisions based on stories and anecdotes rather than a sober analysis of the facts – ultimately are down to our hard-wiring.

That's not to say that we are merely creatures of impulse. From an evolutionary biology perspective, men are programmed to sleep around and generally spread their genetic material as far and wide as much as possible. That may be so, but most men manage to keep that impulse under control, at least most of the time. In the twenty-first century, one stable relationship is likely to lead to greater happiness than a multitude of one-night stands.

Whether as human beings we are able to face the greater challenge of reining back our desire for bigger incomes, greater material wealth and more stuff remains to be seen – but it's certainly a plausible scenario, even if no one can say whether it's a likely one.

Finally, is it possible to have a prosperous economy with zero growth – a steady-state economy?

Adam Smith, the father of modern economics, certainly thought so. Although he's famous for suggesting that individual self-interest and specialisation of labour was the best way to bring economic prosperity to all, he also stated that in the long run, population growth would drive demand that would outstrip the limits of natural resources, and that a period of stability would follow. Writing in the middle of the eighteenth century, he predicted this would take 200 years to happen, so if my scenario comes to pass, he was only 100 years out.

Many other economists have suggested something similar. John Stuart Mill, a hundred years after Adam Smith, wrote:

> the increase of wealth is not boundless. The end of growth leads to a stationary state. The stationary state of capital and wealth ... would be a very considerable improvement on our present condition.

In 2008, former World Bank economist Herman Daly outlined his plan for moving towards what he called a steady-state economy: a world in which is was possible to be prosperous without complete deletion of the natural resources that make prosperity possible. His prescription included a cap and trade system for natural resources, a shift in taxation away from income and towards the taxation of natural resources and pollutants, limits on income inequality and more flexible working practices. A 2009 report from the UK government's Sustainable Development Commission entitled *Prosperity Without Growth* made similar suggestions.

As for going local, a number of key trends point in that direction. These include a move towards home and flexible working, increased transport costs and small-scale power generation from renewables. It's highly likely that the trend towards city living will continue into the twenty-first century. There's been a steady migration to the cities throughout the twentieth century, and it's predicted that by 2030 more than three-quarters of the world's population will live in cities.

It's also true that most cities are more energy-efficient than smaller towns and rural areas. The typical citizen of New York City already has a carbon footprint of one-third that of an average US citizen, mainly because of the lower carbon emissions associated with travel. While the US Congress struggles to agree on even the basic science of climate change, in 2007 New York City's Mayor Michael Bloomberg announced that the city would reduce its greenhouse gas emissions by 30 per cent by 2030, through a combination of cleaner power generation, more energy-efficient businesses, better public transport and a reduction in urban sprawl. The Swedish city of Malmö is on course to reduce its carbon emissions by 50 per cent within ten years, by a systematic programme of working on energy efficiency and renewable power generation district by district. In general, city authorities seem more willing and able to reduce carbon emissions than individuals or national governments.

WHAT DOES THIS MEAN FOR YOUR BUSINESS?

If even some of the elements of this scenario come to pass, it will have major implications for your business. Simply being more energy-efficient won't be enough – you'll have to transform your enterprise into a truly sustainable business if you're to remain competitive in a very different world. You'll need to demonstrate that you're being as resource-efficient as possible throughout your supply chain. You'll need to provide different kinds of products and services in a more locally focused world, some of the products you currently make may need to be offered for rental rather than for sale, and you'll certainly have to accommodate very different working practices, with much more flexible working and part-time working than you're used to at present.

PART IV
What You Need to Do

Although we don't know precisely how the world is going to change as we move towards the low-carbon economy, we know that it will change, and that these changes will present both opportunities and threats for your business. In this part of the book we'll explore how best to capitalise on the opportunities and minimise the threats.

There are five main areas for you to consider. In Chapter 11 we'll look at what you need to be doing to manage energy in your organisation. Under any scenario, energy costs will rise, and if you can't manage energy at least as effectively as your competitors, your company will struggle.

As far as climate change is concerned, it's not energy usage that's the problem – it's the amount of CO_2 and other greenhouse gases that are being put into the atmosphere. More than half of all Fortune 500 companies measure their carbon emissions, and have targets to reduce them: this trend is set to increase as more governments require businesses to manage carbon. Chapter 12 tells you what this means for your business.

Whatever business you're in, changing climate will affect the way you do business, and many companies are already putting plans in place to adapt to a different kind of climate. Chapter 13 explains what you need to do.

For an increasing number of companies and their customers, partners and suppliers, concentrating on just energy and carbon is too narrow a focus. What about other scarce resources like water, wood and plastic? What about pollution and waste? What about the way we treat our employees and suppliers – especially those in developing countries? For these organisations, the goal is to become a truly sustainable company, and we explore what this means in Chapter 14.

Perhaps the biggest opportunities of all in the low-carbon economy are to offer new products and services, and we'll look at this in Chapter 15.

11

Managing Energy

Global energy demand is set to double in the first half of this century, so it's more important than ever that businesses work together to tackle the energy challenge. Human ingenuity and new technology hold the key to unlocking the energy that consumers will need to power their lives in the years ahead.

Gerald Schotman, Chief Technology Officer, Shell

Why Manage Energy?

There are five good reasons for managing your company's energy: it saves money, keeps you legal, improves your reputation, helps engage your staff and is morally right. Let's explore each in turn.

COST

In 2002 a litre of petrol in the UK cost 75p a litre; in 2012 it cost 130p a litre. In 2002 a unit of electricity (1kWh) cost about 5p; in 2012 it cost about 10p. If the rise in energy prices for the next ten years was as steep as the last ten, that would be cause for concern – but as we have seen, under most scenarios the rises will steeper still.

The great thing about reducing your energy costs is that it's very easy to do.

With little investment of time or money, it's easy to make energy savings of 10–20 per cent. Companies that have been willing to make a bigger investment of time and money have found it possible to reduce energy bills by 50 per cent or more. These savings aren't exceptional.

For some organisations, energy is a significant part of their operations, and energy-saving measures can have a big impact on profitability. For others, energy costs are not currently a significant factor in their operations –

even cutting energy bills in half wouldn't make a big impact on the bottom line. Even if energy costs don't have a significant effect on their overall profitability, few companies regret pre-emptive action to reduce their cost base.

REGULATION

In the twentieth century energy was cheap, and there was very little legislation around energy that affected business. At the start of the twenty-first century this started to change, and there are now half a dozen or so significant regulatory constraints on how your business uses energy. Some are simple: the Climate Change Levy is effectively a tax which adds about 8 per cent to the energy bill of every company. Some are more complex: the UK's CRC Energy Efficiency Scheme is also a tax on energy, but it works in a more complicated way. As of 2012 it applies only to large users of energy, roughly those spending more than £500,000 a year on electricity. The scheme may well be rolled out to smaller organisations in the future. Currently, about 27,000 UK companies are registered in the scheme. Each year these businesses must tell the government how much electricity they use, and pay the government accordingly. The scheme was originally called the carbon reduction commitment (hence CRC), and set up as a cap and trade scheme. This meant that companies would buy permits equivalent to the amount of CO_2 produced by the generation of the electricity they used. The government would set a limit – or cap – on the total amount of CO_2 allowable, and this would drive up the cost of permits. Companies which were especially good at reducing their energy costs would get some, or even all, of their money back. When the new coalition government came to power in 2010, it decided to change the scheme from cap and trade to straight taxation.

No one knows exactly how the Climate Change Levy and the CRC Energy Efficiency Scheme will evolve over the coming years, but with growing concerns about climate change and the need for the government to balance its books in a decade of austerity, you can be sure that ever more companies will be asked to pay ever higher taxes for their energy consumption.

Some other regulations are relevant to only a minority of businesses: the European Emissions Trading Scheme is a cap and trade scheme that applies only to very large emitters of greenhouse gases – typically big power stations and very energy-intensive industries like cement and steel production.

REPUTATION

According to a 2011 survey by BrandZ, a global brand analysis firm, more than 90 per cent of consumers want businesses to commit to 3 per cent per annum cuts in greenhouse gas emissions, year on year, in order to achieve the government's emissions targets for 2020 and 2050. But only 7 per cent of consumers believe that companies are taking sufficiently robust action to meet those targets. This may merely reflect a general consumer distrust of business, and of course, approving of a company's carbon emission reductions doesn't necessarily translate to buying more of their products and services. However, a company's reputation is an important factor in its overall success, and businesses that are seen to be actively managing their energy use often have a better reputation than those that don't.

ENGAGEMENT

It's nothing new for businesses to try to involve staff at all levels in boosting productivity and cutting costs. Since Toyota first involved shop floor staff in quality circles in the 1960s, active staff engagement has been the key to any successful organisational improvement. Engaging frontline staff in this way has two main advantages: you get better solutions to problems if you involve the people who're closest to them rather than relying on distant managers or even external consultants, and being involved in some kind of project team often has a positive knock-on effect for that person's motivation in their regular job. Energy-saving is the perfect topic for staff engagement: everyone can relate to what's going on, the results are easily measurable, and there's the commitment that comes from securing the future of the planet as well as securing the future of your company.

DOING THE RIGHT THING

Reducing costs, complying with regulations, enhancing reputation and increasing staff engagement are all good, pragmatic reasons for managing energy. The fifth and final reason is because it's the right thing to do. Businesses in the past have made use of some pretty dubious practices: slave labour in eighteenth-century sugar plantations in the USA and twentieth-century engineering firms in Nazi Germany, child labour in nineteenth-century cotton mills in Manchester and twentieth-century sports shoe manufacturers in India. Most businesses don't do this any more (at least knowingly) because it's wrong. Whether it would be advantageous to employ slave labour (keeping costs low) or disadvantageous (bad for reputation) shouldn't enter into it: it's simply wrong to do so.

Many business owners feel similarly about managing energy. When energy is in short supply, with negative consequences for some of the poorest people in the world, managing energy is simply the right thing to do.

How to Manage Energy

FOCUSING YOUR ATTENTION

Most businesses are big users of energy in three main areas – electricity, heating and transport. Where should you focus your attention?

The best place to start is usually electricity: it's easy to measure, affects everyone in your business, and substantial savings can be made without any capital investment. You probably already monitor your electricity usage on a daily basis, but if you don't, now's the time to begin.

Next on the list is heating, which may be powered by gas or electricity. It's easy to measure your heating bills, and heating affects everyone. Although you can make some easy changes – for example, checking that offices, shops and factories are not heated when there's no one using them – many significant savings in heating (and cooling) will require some capital investment.

Transport should probably be third on your list of energy-saving priorities, unless it forms a substantial part of your company's running costs, as it does with logistics firms and many retailers. It doesn't affect everyone directly, as electricity and heating do, and you have to be far more ingenious to produce substantial savings.

Having decided on your focus of attention, the next step is access good data about your current consumption of energy. Most organisations already have access to this information, although it may be buried in the small detail of your management information system. Most commercial premises will have an electricity meter that provides data every half hour, while many buildings will have some kind of energy management system that gives real-time data on different kinds of energy use. Even if your building is very small and has neither of these, it's easy and cheap to purchase a system that can transmit real-time information on energy usage from your electricity meter to your a computer.

The more frequently you can update this information, the easier it will be to bring about substantial change. When Tesco installed touchscreen energy monitors in the staff areas of nine stores, allowing staff to see which areas of the store were using the most energy, energy usage dropped by 2–3 per cent – a significant saving in a business that uses huge amounts of energy. Tesco is now rolling the system out to a further 500 stores.

While your company's management information processes will provide data on transport costs, you may have access to this information only monthly, or even quarterly. With a small transport operation, this may be sufficiently frequent to make worthwhile savings. With a larger transport operation, you may want to consider something more sophisticated. Most logistics firms track the position of their fleet with GPS (Global Positioning System) technology. It's fairly straightforward to extend this to real-time fuel usage. Eliminating idling times when lorries are waiting to be loaded or unloaded can lead to big savings.

For organisations that do not have a logistics component, business travel, especially by car, is likely to be a major energy consumer. The starting point is once again to gather as accurate and frequent data as possible in order to see what savings can be made.

BEHAVIOURAL CHANGE

Which wastes more energy – a computer or an electric kettle? A computer certainly uses less power than a kettle, but the question was about wasted energy. Computers waste a lot of energy because they're often left on when they're not being used, and kettles waste a lot of energy because they're usually overfilled. In both cases, though, it's people's behaviour that wastes the energy – leaving the computer running when unused, overfilling the kettle.

The first port of call for any business wanting to manage its energy usage has to be to change behaviour. It's the best place to start: partly because it's a great way to engage staff, partly because it requires little or nothing in the way of upfront investment, and partly because many other investments are wasted if you don't get the behavioural change to go with them. A super-efficient heating system will cost you more money if staff leave doors open or override the thermostat because they feel a bit chilly.

An effective programme of behavioural change around energy usage will typically reduce energy bills by 10–20 per cent.

There are different approaches to bringing about behavioural change. You can simply set targets in different parts of your organisation for reducing energy usage: the Co-operative Group found that it was able to reduce energy bills in its food business simply by making setting energy reduction targets for the managers in each of its 3,000 foodstores. In situations where not much attention has been paid to energy in the past, simply setting targets and focusing attention can produce some quick wins. As with any target-based approach, it's important to give people frequent and accurate feedback on how they're progressing towards their target; in the Co-op's case, this was by ensuring store managers could easily manage data from the electricity meters in each store, which recorded energy consumption every half hour.

Many organisations ask for volunteers to be green champions – people who take responsibility for reducing energy consumption in a particular team or location. Sometimes this approach is very informal – green champions volunteer and do what they can. Sometimes it's more structured: green champions are given some basic training in energy efficiency and some tips on how to influence the behaviour of others. The effectiveness of green champions depends very much on their individual personality – the successful ones are genuinely committed, understand the issues, and most importantly, have credibility with their working colleagues. When green champions are ineffective, it's often the credibility issue that is at stake. One green champion in small business wanted to encourage more employees to cycle to work. In order to set an example, he began cycling a 20-mile round trip to work in all weathers. He was extremely disappointed that no one followed his example. The problem was that he lacked credibility with his fellow employees. In the eyes of his colleagues, anyone who was mad enough to cycle 20 miles a day in rain and even snow was obviously too fanatical about this green stuff to be trusted on anything.

Perhaps the most effective way to bring about behavioural change is to use project teams. I'll go into much more detail on how to use project teams to bring about all kinds of organisational change in Part V of this book, but suffice to say for now that the successful project teams have clear objectives, are properly resourced, and are made up of people who are credible, competent and committed.

ENERGY-SAVING DEVICES

The two main approaches to energy saving are to turn off equipment, lights and heating systems when not in use, and to use more energy-efficient equipment, lights and heating systems.

You can influence people to turn off unused equipment, or you can get the equipment to turn itself off. Motion detectors on lights, for example, will automatically switch off the lights when there's no on moving about in the room, and software on computers can power down the computer when no one's using it.

Sometimes redesigning the way equipment is used can save energy. The food industry uses a lot of compressed air to move things around. Energy savings are to be found both by reducing leakages in compressed air systems and by pre-drying the air – dry air compresses faster and more easily than moisture-laden air. Manufacturing companies rely on a lot of electrically powered presses and machine tools. Voltage-regulating equipment can ensure that the minimum amount of power is used by the machine at each stage in the process. This not only reduces energy costs, but prevents excess energy being turned into heat – which would in turn require more energy for air conditioning.

Sometimes equipment can be retrofitted to save energy. A typical industrial heating boiler, for example, wastes a lot of energy turning itself on and off at the request of a thermostat. Sabien Technologies produces a small gadget that attaches to a boiler. By controlling how the boiler powers up and down, energy costs can be reduced by 10–25 per cent. Sophisticated energy management systems for whole buildings and sites can produce similar savings.

Almost anything that uses energy in an office, shop or factory can be replaced by a low-energy alternative. Compact fluorescent lighting uses a third of the power of a traditional incandescent bulb. LED lighting uses a tenth of the power of a traditional incandescent. An efficient gas boiler uses a third of the power of a traditional boiler. A modern computer uses half the power of a typical five-year-old model.

HEATING, COOLING AND BUILDINGS

Around 20 per cent of all energy consumed in the UK is for commercial properties, principally for lighting and heating buildings. You can make existing buildings more energy-efficient with better insulation in roofs, walls and windows. If you rent a building, your landlord may not have an immediate incentive for making the building more energy-efficient. This may change. A 2009 study by the UK's Royal Institution of Chartered Surveyors found that sustainable buildings are increasingly viewed as more valuable than traditional office stock. In a study of US office buildings, those with the LEED (Leadership in Energy and Environmental Design) certification were valued at 16 per cent more than their conventional counterparts. As energy prices continue to rise, these differentials are likely to increase.

For many companies, it makes sense to move to a new, more energy-efficient building. Most commercial and domestic buildings in the UK are required to have an Energy Performance Certificate (EPC) when they're constructed, rented or sold. This grades the energy efficiency of the building on a scale from A (the highest) to G (the lowest). The EPC also shows the potential energy performance of a building if certain energy-saving measures are taken. Although there's no direct correlation between building regulations and EPC certification for new build, in practice most new office buildings will be built to an EPC A or B certification.

The gold standard in energy efficiency is BREEAM, the Building Research Establishment Environmental Assessment Model. In addition to energy efficiency, the standard also considers water usage, the materials used in the building's construction, and the health impact on users, in terms of things like air quality and daylight.

MAKING YOUR OWN POWER

If you're concerned about the rising costs of energy and secure energy supplies for your business, why not generate your own power? This comes in three varieties: generating your own electricity, generating your own heat, and combined heat and power.

Until very recently, it made little business sense for any organisation to generate its own power. With cheap fossil fuels and the economies of scale to be had from large power stations, it was uneconomic for most businesses to want to generate their own power. Why tie up a lot of capital in your own source of power if it was more expensive per unit of energy than plugging into the grid?

Since then, things have changed. As fossil fuel prices have gone up, so the cost of energy from small-scale renewables has dropped, and concerns about energy security and climate change have resulted in governments subsidising the cost of locally generated electricity, through a system known as Feed-in Tariffs. If you install a source of renewable energy, the government will pay you for every unit of electricity you produce, even if you use that electricity yourself. If you choose not to use it, but to export it back to the grid, the government pays you a bit more. The amount you're paid depends on when you first enrol in the scheme, which form of renewable you use, and how big the installation is. Eligible technologies include solar photovoltaics, wind power and hydroelectricity. In 2012, the UK scheme is fairly generous, but the rates will decline and may disappear entirely in 2013, when the scheme will be reviewed.

Similar to the Feed-in Tariff scheme is the Renewable Heat Incentive (RHI), which started in the UK in 2011. If you install a hot water or heating system based on renewable energy, the government will pay you a guaranteed index-linked sum for the next 20 years for each unit of heat you produce. The precise rate once again depends on when you first get involved in the scheme, which form of renewable you use, and how big the system is. In 2012, eligible technologies include solar thermal, heat pumps and biomass boilers.

Whereas the UK has very much followed the pack with FITs, already in use in 40 other countries when introduced into the UK, the Renewable Heat Incentive is a world first for the UK. Because there is no national grid of heat, there are no RHI payments for exporting the excess heat you produce.

Straddling the electricity and heat-generation markets is combined heat and power (CHP). Half of all the energy generated in a typical large power station is lost, mainly as waste heat in a cooling tower. If you generate the electricity closer to where it's being used, you avoid the losses in transmission and you could use that heat for something useful. Large-scale CHP schemes have been around for many years. Seven power stations in Manhattan, New York also supply steam heating to about 100,000 commercial and residential buildings in the city, which is why you often see steam rising from manhole covers in movie scenes from New York.

Smaller-scale CHP – also called cogeneration – is relatively new to the UK, but an increasing number of businesses are using it, especially as it can be subsidised through the Renewable Heat Incentive. Most CHP schemes are fuelled by gas, although they can also use biomass or biofuels. The major drawback of CHP is that your need for heat doesn't always correspond to your production of it. Nevertheless, it's worth exploring for big energy users.

FLEXIBLE WORKING

If office costs are a significant part of your organisation's overheads, the most effective way to make a big reduction in your energy usage and costs isn't to make your office more energy-efficient, it's to stop employees coming into the office at all.

Of course, not all jobs are suitable for this kind of flexible working. Jobs that involve serving members of the public or operating equipment in factories are clearly location-based. But you only have to look at the number of empty desks in a typical office to realise that paying for every office-based employee to have their own desk all the time is a very inefficient way to run a business. Average desk occupancy in the UK for full-time office-based workers is 40–50 per cent.

It's sometimes said that flexible working doesn't really reduce energy consumption, it merely transfers the bills from the company to the individual homeworker. In practice, it costs a great deal more to heat and light a desk in an office building, with all the accompanying paraphernalia of reception areas, lifts and communal areas, than it does to heat and light a home office. Remember too that flexible working greatly reduces travel to and from the workplace, and commuting represents a large proportion of all travel.

Flexible working, by its nature, is different for every individual and each different function within an organisation. Some jobs may be able to be done entirely remotely, while others may require some attendance at the office or in other locations. A study by Richard Lepsinger into the effectiveness of virtual teams – teams who did not work together in the same physical location – found that virtual teams that had some face-to-face meetings early on in the team's life generally delivered superior results to those who never met in the real world.

If flexible working is to succeed in your organisation, you have to ensure that three things are in place.

Firstly, every member of staff must have the opportunity to negotiate with his or her manager about how flexibly they'll work. How often will they be expected to work from home, from an office desk or from some other location? This negotiation should take into account three factors: the requirements of the job, the individual's personal preferences, and the individual's home circumstances.

Secondly, the managers in your business must learn how to manage for results, not effort. They must learn how to agree what each flexible worker in their team will deliver by way of results, and how this is to be measured and monitored. Even if your business has a sophisticated approach to performance management, it's likely that some of your managers are good at keeping an eye on the people when they're physically present, but not so good at managing remotely.

Thirdly, you must ensure that staff are equipped with the skills to work more independently. Most people love to work flexibly when they're used to it, but it does take some adjustment. A tiny minority never make the transition.

Energy Management in Practice

IN THE OFFICE

The Co-operative Group employs around 123,000 people in the UK, in businesses ranging from banking and funeral care to pharmacies and food. In 2006, with energy bills and concerns about climate change both rising rapidly, the Co-op decided to take action. The initial focus was on their most intensive use of energy, at their head office in Manchester and in their national network of 3,000 foodstores. By 2010, energy consumption had been cut to 29 per cent of 2006 levels, by a combination of behavioural change, a store refit programme and some specific initiatives at the most energy-intensive stores.

Although it provides a workplace for only 4,000 staff, the Co-op's Manchester HQ is very energy-intensive, consisting as it does of a collection of buildings from the Victorian era up to the 1960s, none of which was built with energy efficiency in mind. None of them was well suited to being the HQ of a modern business.

The Co-op therefore took the decision to build a completely new head office building, to the highest environmental standards, which in 2012 is the BREEAM Outstanding rating. The building will maintain this rating when it is fully in use from 2013 onwards. A double-skinned glass façade will maximise natural lighting and control heat gain in the winter and heat loss in the summer. Most of the building's energy requirements will be provided by an onsite combined heat and power plant, fuelled by plant oil grown on the Co-op's farms. Rainwater and greywater recycling will minimise water usage. The new building will save the Co-op more than £500,000 a year in energy and water costs. In line with the Co-op's strong social values, the building is not a standalone project, but part of a joint venture with Manchester City Council called NOMA, to regenerate an area of Northern Manchester.

The biggest energy savings of all will come not from the building's design, but from the way it's used. Few staff will have a permanent desk in the new building. Most will work flexibly, varying their working base between home, the new office and local Co-op stores. As Chief Executive Peter Marks explains, this will be a culture change for the Co-op.

> We still have lots of individual offices, limited collaboration by and between teams, and a culture that puts too much emphasis on time spent at work rather than the outputs being achieved. If we're going to help our colleagues become a modern, effective workforce, we have to start changing our ways of working.

IN THE SHOP

Tesco is the third largest food retailer in the world and the largest in the UK, with a £60 billion annual turnover, 5,300 stores and 472,000 employees. Like all food retailers, it is a big user of energy. Tesco aims to reduce its overall carbon footprint by 50 per cent by 2020, and to be an entirely carbon-neutral company by 2050.

Tesco reduced its energy usage in stores by 50 per cent between 2000 and 2008 by focusing on three main areas. The first is refrigeration, a big user of energy in its stores. Simply redesigning the shape of fridges to keep more cool air in saves 10 per cent on energy costs. The second is heating, in particular by recovering waste heat from ovens and directing it to heat the store. The third area is lighting, using more energy-efficient lighting and motion sensors to turn lights off when they're not being used in storerooms and offices.

Reducing energy usage is easier with a new build than it is when retrofitting existing stores, and Tesco has made even further progress with its new stores. Its recently opened store in Ramsey, Cambridgeshire produces no carbon emissions in its operations. Unlike many traditional supermarkets, much of the lighting is from natural daylight, using gel-filled window panels that allow in light, but not much heat. As natural daylight increases, electric lighting automatically dims. The car park is lit by LEDs. Roof vents provide natural ventilation and much reduce the need for air conditioning. The store has its own power plant, using recycled vegetable oils as fuel. It's a CHP plant, which means that the heat produced in generating electricity is used to heat the store. Although the store is more or less self-sufficient in energy, it's linked to the grid so that it can sell electricity when in-store demand is low and buy it from the grid when demand is high. The overall energy costs of the store are less than 30 per cent of a conventional store of similar size.

IN THE SMALL FACTORY

Warren Evans is a small bed and furniture manufacturer employing 90 people. In 2006 the firm moved from three locations near Central London to a new workshop in Walthamstow to the east of London. This was an opportunity for the firm to take close look at how it was operating, and how it could not only reduce its energy costs, but become more sustainable. By examining the flow of work through the factory, the time per bed was reduced by 11 per cent and the cost of wood per bed by 6 per cent, despite a 20 per cent rise in the cost of raw materials. Instead of paying for scrap wood to be taken to landfill, the company installed a biomass burner which now provides heating for the factory. Of all the companies in the Time 100 list of best green companies, Warren Evans scored top for employee engagement.

IN THE LARGE FACTORY

Cargill is an international producer of food and agricultural products, employing over 138,000 staff in 63 countries, and reducing environmental impact and conserving natural resources is one of it four key business commitments. Its wheat processing plant in Manchester turns 750,000 tonnes of wheat annually into sweeteners, proteins for the baking industry and dairy feed ingredients, using a lot of energy along the way. Energy efficiency is a core facet of everyone's job, from the engineers who ensure that the drive shafts in electric motors are perfectly aligned, thereby reducing wear and electricity bills, to office staff who set up a bicycle user group to promote alternatives to driving to work. The biggest energy savings have come from process mapping and CHP.

Many of Cargill's industrial processes involve heating things up and cooling them down – both of which use energy. By redesigning processes, they were able to reduce the overall amount of heating and cooling, reuse waste heat, and reduce energy bills by £800,000. They saved a similar amount by installing CHP to provide both electricity and steam.

IN THE DATA CENTRE

Some 1.5 per cent of all the electricity consumed in the world in 2012 was used by just one kind of 'factory' – the computer data centre. Computers not only require a fair bit of energy to run, they also don't like being too hot, so some form of cooling is essential. A typical data centre uses as much power for cooling and lighting as it does to power the computers themselves.

One of the world's biggest owners of data centres is, unsurprisingly, Google. Many of its huge data centres use half the power of a typical data centre, largely through innovative cooling techniques. Its Hamina, Finland data centre uses seawater from the Bay of Finland to keep the servers cool, while its new Dublin server farm will be air-cooled instead of using conventional air conditioning units.

12

Managing Carbon

One reason we use energy so lavishly today is that the price of energy does not include all of the social costs of producing it. The costs incurred in protecting the environment and the health and safety of workers, for example, are part of the real costs of producing energy – but they are not now all included in the price of the product.
Richard Nixon, President of the United States, in 1971

If human beings continue to put large quantities of CO_2 and other greenhouse gases into the atmosphere, the world will continue to get warmer. Most scientists and most national governments think that a little bit of warming is OK. Too much warming, though – more than 2°C – could be bad, very bad, or even catastrophic. That's why many countries have set targets for reducing CO_2 emissions. In the UK the goal is a 34 per cent reduction by 2020 and an 80 per cent reduction by 2050 (measured against a 1990 baseline), and most European countries have similar targets. But as any business leader knows, you have to measure progress towards a target if you want to have any chance of hitting it. That's why governments, and people who are concerned about climate change, are very keen that businesses measure their CO_2 and other greenhouse gas emissions; in the UK it's already mandatory for some very large organisations to do so.

Managing carbon means measuring your CO_2 and other greenhouse gas emissions and taking active steps to reduce them, in the same way that managing energy means measuring your energy usage and taking steps to reduce it. But managing carbon is nowhere near as straightforward as managing energy.

Although we talk about 'managing carbon' and 'CO_2 emissions', CO_2 isn't the only greenhouse gas. Methane and nitrous oxide are even more potent greenhouse gases than CO_2. When we say 'managing carbon', this is really shorthand for 'managing CO_2 and all the other greenhouse gases'.

It's conventional to use a measure called CO_2e – the amount of carbon dioxide that would produce an equivalent amount of climate change to that produced by the greenhouse gases in question. A cow, for example, produces 3 tonnes per annum of CO_2e carbon emissions – about the same as an average family car. Although it produces a little CO_2 (from breathing), most of the cow's carbon footprint is due to the methane which the cow produces as it digests its food. As methane is 25 times more effective at trapping heat than CO_2, the cow doesn't need to produce a great deal of methane to hit the 3 tonnes CO_2e. The terms 'carbon emissions' and 'greenhouse gas emissions' are usually used to mean the same thing, although technically speaking CO_2 is only one of many greenhouse gases.

One very crude way to measure the carbon footprint of your business is to base it on your energy usage. If you take electricity from the national grid, which is mainly powered by conventional coal- and gas-fired power stations, every 2kWh of energy you use means 1 kilogram of CO_2e has been released into the air. If you use gas for heating, every 5kWh of energy used for heating has resulted in 1 kilogram of CO_2e. One kWh of electricity produces more CO_2e than 1kWh of gas heating because burning gas produces less CO_2e than burning coal, and we still use a lot of coal in the UK for electricity generation. Also, when you burn gas in your factory, office or store, most of the energy is useful heat; when you burn coal or gas in a power station, half the energy is wasted in heat and only half gets turned into electricity. If your company is large enough to be part of the UK CRC scheme, this is the way your carbon footprint's measured – or at least it was in 2012. As a larger percentage of the UK's power comes from renewable sources, you'd expect the conversion factors between kWh of electricity and CO_2e emissions to change.

Defining the Scope of Your Carbon Emissions

Scope 1 emissions are greenhouse gas emissions produced by the business onsite. Many businesses don't have any Scope 1 emissions to speak of, unless they use gas for heating. Most farms, however, have substantial Scope 1 emissions, because most livestock produces a lot of methane, and fields leach nitrous oxide into the air from the nitrogen-based fertilisers that nearly every (non-organic) farm uses.

Scope 2 emissions are the greenhouse gas emissions that have been produced by the business's use of energy that has been purchased offsite. For most businesses, this means electricity.

Taken together, Scope 1 and Scope 2 emissions are sometimes referred to as the *operational carbon footprint* of the business. When businesses claim to be carbon-neutral, they usually mean operationally carbon-neutral.

But most companies are in some sense also responsible for other carbon emissions outside the immediate business. Consider your local foodstore. Its operational carbon footprint is fairly modest, mainly from heating and lighting. But if you think about growing the food and transporting it from the farm to depot to store, the carbon footprint starts to look a lot bigger. And if you also include the transport from the store to the customer's home, the energy used to store and cook it, and the methane that is produced after waste food is dumped in landfill, the carbon footprint becomes bigger again.

Measuring this kind of carbon footprint along the whole supplier–customer chain, is Scope 3. This is sometimes called the *full carbon footprint* of the business, product or activity. To see what this means in practice, let's look at the Scope 3 emissions for a single product – a packet of crisps.

According to Walkers Crisps, growing the potatoes and the sunflowers (used to make sunflower oil for frying) one packet of crisps produces, on average 29 grams' worth of greenhouse gases. Where has this 29 grams of CO_2 come from? Growing potatoes uses a lot of fertiliser, and making fertiliser uses a lot of energy. Fertiliser also releases nitrous oxide, another greenhouse gas, when it is sprinkled onto the field, and tractors use energy when the potato crop is planted and harvested.

Producing the packaging for a bag of crisps produces 27 grams CO_2e – almost as much as growing the food inside. It takes quite a lot of energy to turn oil into plastic, and a bit more energy to shape the plastic into a crisp packet.

You'd think frying the spuds and turning them into crisps would take quite a lot of energy, but the carbon footprint for this part of the process is a surprisingly low 14 grams CO_2e. The transport involved at the various stages of the process adds another 8 grams CO_2e. Unlike some products – cars, for example – crisps don't generate any greenhouse gases while they're 'in use', but disposing of the empty packets at the end adds another 2 grams CO_2e, making a grand total of 80 grams CO_2e.

Calculating the carbon footprint of anything isn't an exact science. Depending on where they're finally purchased, some packets of crisps may travel much further than others; some farms may be more efficient at growing potatoes than others. And what do you include? Should you include the carbon footprint of the deep-fat fryers used to make the crisps? (Probably.) Should you include the carbon footprint of the car journey from the supermarket where they are bought to the house where they're eaten? (Probably not.)

As there are no simple answers to these questions, it would be useful to have some kind of standard way of reporting carbon emissions – and fortunately there is. A not-for-profit organisation called the Carbon Disclosure Project (CDP) has a standard way of measuring the carbon footprints of different kinds of business. At the time of writing in 2012, over 3,000 organisations in over 60 countries choose to measure and report their carbon emissions to the CDP, and the number is increasing each day. Given the complexity in measuring and reporting carbon, why do they bother?

Why Manage Carbon?

The reasons for managing carbon are the same as the reasons for managing energy – cost, regulation, reputation, engagement and doing the right thing.

COST

According to a 2011 report from the Carbon Disclosure Project, more than 50 per cent of firms and 25 per cent of their suppliers have made cost savings as a result of carbon footprinting activities. PepsiCo, for example, identified $60 million of energy savings across its beverage businesses as a result of mapping the carbon emissions across its supply chain. Of the 500 companies mentioned in the report, 59 per cent of investments in emissions reductions – mostly energy efficiency or renewable energy – paid for themselves within three years.

When Walkers looked at the supply chain for its crisps, one of its interesting observations was that farmers tended to store potatoes in quite damp conditions. Farmers were paid so much per tonne of potato, and because moist potatoes weigh more than dry ones, there was a financial incentive for farmers to continue selling slightly moist spuds. But this caused Walkers problems at the crisp factory – damp potatoes require more energy to turn into crisps than drier ones. Walkers agreed to pay the farmers a slightly higher price per tonne if the potatoes were stored in a drier environment (which the farmers liked) because this reduced the energy costs of frying them into crisps (which Walkers liked). Arguably, Walkers could have made this cost saving by conducting a rigorous cost analysis of every part of its supply chain, but it was a clear spin-off from analysing the carbon footprint.

REGULATION

Although many countries in the world already oblige large organisations to measure and report on carbon emissions, the requirement is usually only to report on Scope 1 and 2 emissions – that is to say, operational carbon. Many governments are considering extending this both to smaller organisations and to measure Scope 3 emissions too.

Under the terms of the UK's 2008 Climate Change Act, the government is obliged to introduce some form of mandatory carbon disclosure by 2012, or give Parliament some good reasons why it has chosen not to do so. At the time of writing, it's not clear just what the government will choose to do about carbon disclosure, and who will be affected.

The arguments in favour of mandatory reporting are as follows. Many businesses already report carbon emissions: 70 per cent of FTSE 350 companies already report to the Carbon Disclosure Project on a voluntary basis. In January 2010 a group of businesspeople and institutional investors signed an open letter urging the UK government to introduce mandatory reporting as soon as possible. The group included Aviva, AXA Investment Managers, Biffa, BT, Centrica, Jupiter, Microsoft, National Grid, Pepsico UK, Siemens, Scottish and Southern Energy, the Co-operative Group, Veolia and Willmott Dixon. The presence of investors on this list is particularly interesting, as they see carbon reporting and management as a source of competitive advantage. Finally, if the government is serious about achieving its carbon reduction targets, it's hard to see how this can come about unless businesses start measuring and reducing their carbon emissions.

The argument against mandatory reporting is that is places an additional administrative burden on business. The current UK coalition government is both philosophically opposed to business regulation and not very focused on what are perceived to be 'green' issues. It remains to be seen whether it becomes mandatory to measure carbon emissions, and if so, what form this might take.

REPUTATION

Whether your company is a one-person start-up or a well-established multinational, you need investors to sustain and grow your organisation, and investors like to see the numbers. As issues of climate change and sustainability move higher up the business agenda, investors want reassurance that you're not only measuring your carbon footprint, but taking active steps to reduce it. One of the Carbon Disclosure Project's specialist programmes provides information to over 500 institutional investors. Every corporate investor wants to minimise risk in their investment, and companies which don't manage carbon are at risk not only from future legislation, but from shifts in customer perception as sustainability become more of a mainstream business issue.

An increasing number of the world's largest business customers are asking their suppliers to demonstrate their sustainable credentials. Every Walmart supplier, for example, has to answer a supplier checklist, of which the first two questions are:

1.   Have you measured and taken steps to reduce your corporate greenhouse gas emissions?
2.   Have you opted to report your greenhouse gas emissions and climate change strategy to the Carbon Disclosure Project?

Suppliers are not automatically disqualified if they give negative answers to these questions, but it does affect the chances of a long-term relationship with Walmart. In March 2011, BT announced its new procurement policy, which takes a similar approach, by asking its 6,000 suppliers to measure, report and reduce their carbon footprints.

ENGAGEMENT

Some of your employees take a fairly transactional view of coming to work. They don't much care about what the company does or how it does it: as long as they're paid fairly and the work isn't too dull or too stressful, they'll continue to be good employees. But others take a very different view of work. They want their work to give them some sense of purpose, and they want to work for a company that operates in an ethical and fair way. This may be a generational issue. The baby boomers, who began their working lives in the 1970s and 1980s, didn't particularly expect work to be fulfilling or conducted in a particularly ethical way. When the character of Gordon Gekko in the 1987 movie *Wall Street* expressed the sentiment that 'greed is good', it was a fairly accurate summary of how many large organisations were run at the time.

In the wake of the 2008–2009 financial crisis there's a lot more debate about what businesses are really for, and right on cue, Generation Y – people entering the workforce about now – are much more concerned about the purpose and ethics of the organisations they work for than ever before. Of course, it's possible to measure your carbon emissions and still be a terrible organisation, but in the minds of many people – and not just the youngest generation – a company that wants to manage its greenhouse gas emissions is likely to be a company that has a sense of purpose and wants to operate in an ethical way. Such a company will find it much easier to recruit and engage talent than one that focuses simply on shareholder return.

DOING THE RIGHT THING

In 2011, consulting firm Accenture asked almost 250 board-level executives in a range of UK, US and Chinese companies about sustainability initiatives, which were primarily focused on reducing carbon emissions. The key focus of the study was on how successful these initiatives had been. Seventy-two per cent reported that these initiatives has exceeded expectations in terms of delivering a financial payback. What was interesting about the study was the motivation for these sustainability initiatives. While it's widely accepted that sustainability projects are driven by a need to reduce costs, comply with legislation, enhance reputation and increase employee engagement, this research found that the top motivation for these initiatives was actually none of these – it was instead given as a genuine concern for environment and society. In other words, while business leaders can see the positive impact on the bottom line from reducing greenhouse gas emissions, the motivation to do so was often a desire to do the right thing.

Footprinting Food

Booths is a small independent chain of supermarkets based in the North West of England. The current chairman, Edwin Booth, is the great-great-grandson of the firm's founder, also an Edwin Booth. Although it faces ruthless competition from the UK's large supermarket chains, especially Tesco, Asda, Sainsbury's and Morrisons, it's managed to carve out a strong reputation and a loyal customer base. Its commitment to customer service, innovation and sustainability has won it many awards.

In 2008 it commissioned specialist carbon footprinting firm Small World Consulting to analyse the company's overall carbon footprint, and the results were published in 2010. The annual carbon footprint of Booths and its product supply chains is estimated to be 226,000 tonnes of CO_2e per year. Of this, 67 per cent is caused by growing the food, involving as it does large quantities of nitrous oxide (in fertilisers) and methane (from livestock). The next largest slice, at 12 per cent, is produced by heating and lighting the stores and offices. Staff transport is also included in this chunk.

Transport of goods is the next largest slice, at 9 per cent. Of the transport emissions, two-thirds are from road freight – most Booths products make at least two journeys by road, from the docks or a UK farm to its distribution depot, and from the depot to the store. But most of the remaining two-thirds is accounted for by the very small number of products that are – or rather were – air freighted. Most of the produce from outside the UK travels by ship, and this accounted for just 7 per cent of the transport total. Packaging is the next biggest contributor to greenhouse gases, at 7 per cent. Food processing and storage, at 5 per cent, complete the picture.

In order to assess the carbon footprint of the whole company, it was necessary to estimate the carbon footprint the whole of the company's product range, broken down into 77 product categories, and by life cycle stage within each. As well as identifying the absolute carbon footprint of the various products sold, Booths also looked at the carbon-intensity of it various products – how much greenhouse gas was produced per £1 of retail value.

The most carbon-intensive food category at Booths is meat. Because shoppers like to buy a lot of meat and animal products, the meat and fish category accounts for a quarter of Booths' entire carbon footprint. Why is meat – especially beef and lamb – so carbon-intensive? Partly because animals use a lot of energy, wandering around and keeping warm, and this energy has to come from somewhere. In practice, it comes from animal feed, which in turn requires fertilisers and energy to grow. In addition, cows and sheep produce methane from their digestive systems, and methane is a very potent greenhouse gas.

Switching to a vegetarian diet does significantly reduce the carbon footprint of a diet, particularly if plant-based foods are substituted for meat. The carbon-intensity of eggs and dairy products sold at Booths are a bit lower than meat, but higher than almost any other food category. Eggs and dairy products are ultimately derived from animals, so their carbon footprint remains high.

If you want to reduce your carbon footprint by changing your diet, eliminating meat and animal products in favour of a diet of vegetables and pulses would be best, providing you choose the right vegetables. Booths discovered a big difference between the carbon footprint of the vast majority of their vegetables (which was generally very low) and a small selection of vegetables that were either air freighted or hothoused – that is, grown in heated greenhouses. For most of us, the simplest way of reducing our impact would be to cut down on the food we waste.

As a result of this analysis, Booths has embarked on a series of actions that will reduce its overall carbon footprint. One of the largest contributors to CO_2 within stores is refrigeration, and switching to more efficient CO_2-based fridges will save 8,400 tonnes of CO_2e a year – almost 4 per cent of Booths' entire total. Other initiatives focus on reducing waste within stores, better packaging, better transport (including smarter scheduling and training drivers in fuel-efficient driving) and better product sourcing, avoiding air freighting and hothousing where possible. Perhaps the most important change is the emphasis Booths is now placing on its more sustainable fruit and vegetable products: anything seasonal or shipped from a sunny climate.

Carbon Labelling

Booth's motivation for analysing the carbon footprint of its products was primarily to understand and reduce the company's overall carbon footprint. But businesses like Booths that sell directly to consumers may soon find that there is another rationale for measuring the carbon footprint of individual products: carbon labelling.

Some 100 French companies are now taking part in a pilot carbon labelling scheme, involving a range of products from food to furniture, clothes to cleaning products. In some stores belonging to supermarket group E Leclerc, not only is the carbon footprint of every product displayed on the shelf alongside its price, but the till receipt will tell you carbon footprint of your trolley load and how it compares to the average. This pilot labelling scheme may well lead to compulsory carbon labelling in France by around 2013.

Although different organisations measure the carbon footprint of a product in difference ways, a global standard is emerging based on a benchmark called PAS 2050, which was first developed by the UK's Carbon Trust. It's likely to be adopted by the Greenhouse Gas Protocol, a joint project of the World Resources Institute and the World Business Council for Sustainable Development.

According to Daniel Goleman, author of *Ecological Intelligence*, consumer choices the world over will be increasingly influenced by the way products are made – which includes their carbon footprint – as well as the cost and perceived quality. Even if you choose not to put this kind of information on the label, this doesn't mean that consumers won't be able to find out. It's already possible to use a free app on your smartphone to give you instant information about environmental aspects of over 120,000 products. You simply scan the product's bar code, and the information appears.

Becoming Carbon-neutral and Offsetting

If you book a ticket to travel from London to Paris with train company Eurostar, you'll discover that not only does Eurostar train travel generate a tenth of the emissions of flying, but your journey's carbon-neutral. What does this mean, and how can these two facts be reconciled?

According to the Eurostar website, a return trip from London to Paris by Eurostar generates 6.6 kilograms CO_2e per passenger, in comparison with a return flight from London Luton to Paris Charles de Gaulle, which generates 102.8 kilograms CO_2e. Not only are trains significantly more energy-efficient than aircraft, but Eurostar has two significant advantages – its trains tend to be fairly consistently full, whereas many planes often fly half-empty, and because a lot of Eurostar's mileage is in France, it can benefit from France's low-carbon nuclear power to drive its electric trains. The company has also put a lot of effort into measuring, and reducing its carbon footprint. Between 2007 and 2010 Eurostar reduced its CO_2 emissions per traveller by 25 per cent through a combination of sourcing energy from less carbon-intensive sources, better driving techniques and more efficient onboard lighting and heating.

All well and good – but how can it claim that its journeys are actually carbon-neutral? This is achieved through the use of offsetting. In a nutshell, offsetting means that you pay someone else to reduce their carbon emissions by the same amount as the carbon emissions you yourself produce. When it comes to global warming, the atmosphere doesn't care whether the reduction of 100,000 tonnes of CO_2 comes from fewer trains between London and Paris or from replacing one coal-fired power station in India with a hydroelectric power plant. What matters is that emissions are reduced.

Carbon offsetting is controversial, and there are three main criticisms. The first is usually known as the problem of additionality: how do you know that this Indian hydroelectric power station wasn't going to be built anyway? If you're supporting greenhouse gas reduction projects that would have happened even without your funding, you're not really causing a net decrease in greenhouse gas emissions. The second criticism is that some carbon offset projects never really deliver the benefits promised, and this certainly applied to many projects in the early days of offsetting. The third criticism is that offsetting lets rich Westerners off the hook – why bother reducing your own emissions when you can pay someone else to reduce theirs? Some more cynical commentators have likened offsets to the indulgences sold to the faithful by the medieval Christian Church: purchase an expensive splinter of the true cross and you can buy your way into heaven without actually having to change your behaviour and renounce your vices. Purchase carbon offsets and you can claim to be a sustainable organisation without having to change your behaviour or renounce your profligate use of fossil fuel energy.

However, there are some very positive things about carbon offsets. One of the criticisms of spending money on reducing the emission of greenhouse gases is that there are other things it's more important to spend money on – alleviating poverty, reducing disease and improving education in developing countries, for example. Carbon offsetting, if done well, addresses two issues for the price of one: by funding a clean energy project in a developing country, you're both reducing carbon emissions and supporting local communities in a sustainable way – ultimately, in a way that can address the poverty, disease and lack of education suffered by the poorest billion people on the planet.

You'll have noticed that I used the phrase 'if done well' in relation to offsetting. There are a number of internationally recognised standards for offsetting, including the Voluntary Carbon Standard and the Gold Standard. There are also a number of specialist brokers who can advise companies on which offset projects to invest in. Eurostar worked with a consultancy called Carbon Clear to help identify appropriate offsetting projects. It has invested in windfarms, small-scale hydroelectric power and biomass power plants in India and China.

Banking group HSBC was the first FTSE 100 company to become carbon-neutral. The company estimates that it's responsible for producing around 1 million tonnes of greenhouse gases every year. It works with the United Nations Clean Development mechanism to support projects, mainly in the developing world, to reduce their carbon emissions by an equivalent amount to the million tonnes of CO_2e it produces itself. Hence, the organisation is carbon-neutral.

It's virtually impossible for any mainstream organisation to be carbon-neutral without some form of offsetting, simply because every firm uses energy. At the moment, producing energy usually produces a lot of CO_2. In fifty years' time, if the world's electricity supply has been completely decarbonised and transport is similarly carbon-free and the agricultural industry has found a way to feed us without nitrogen-based fertilisers and methane-emitting livestock, the situation might be different; but for now, the only way to achieve even operational carbon-neutrality is by offsetting.

It's also worth pointing out that achieving carbon-neutrality is a lot easier for some companies than others. Relative to their economic activity, banks don't use a lot of energy – they have to heat and light their offices, power up their computers and move their staff around, and that's about it. Retailers, which have physical goods to shift, use a lot more energy, and manufacturers use even more still. Even if you believed in the value of offsetting, few manufacturers could afford to offset their current operational emissions.

Many companies choose not to become carbon-neutral, at least not in the short term, but instead set themselves some fairly aggressive carbon-reduction targets. The Co-operative Group, for example, which includes banks, supermarkets and farms, reduced its operational greenhouse gas emissions by 35 per cent between 2006 and 2010.

What's a reasonable target to set in order to have credibility as a sustainable organisation? To some extent that depends on the nature of your business and what you've already achieved. The UK's national targets are for a 34 per cent reduction by 2020 and 80 per cent reduction by 2050 (against a 1990 baseline). Achieving or improving on these targets for your business is a good place to start.

13

Adaptation

Climate is an angry beast, and we are poking at it with sticks.
Wallace Broecker, scientist

Whatever you do to manage energy and carbon in your business, the world's climate will continue to warm. As the climate changes, so does the weather – in most places the weather will get warmer and less predictable. In the UK, for example, we can expect warmer, drier summers, milder, wetter winters, and more extreme weather events – very hot spells, very cold spells, flooding and winds.

Weather affects businesses in all kinds of ways. Weather can disrupt logistics and make buildings harder to heat and cool. Weather can prevent employees getting to work and make them lethargic or bad-tempered when they arrive. Weather can disrupt processes and markets, but also open up new opportunities. No business can afford to ignore the weather, and as the effects of climate change become more apparent, no business can afford not to adapt to climate change. In this chapter we'll examine the various threats and opportunities that climate-induced weather changes present to your business, and how to deal with them. But first, why bother? – Why not just wait and see what happens, and deal with it then?

Why Bother?

Kyriacos Akathiotis certainly hadn't even thought about climate change before 2000. In November of that year freak floods caused £175,000 worth of damage to his fish and chip cafe in Bewdley, Worcestershire. His insurance policy excluded flood cover. He's thinking about it now, though: when refitting the shop, the expensive and heavy fryers were mounted on a hydraulic system to raise them above the level of any future flood, and the fridges have their motors set on top rather than below for the same reason.

There are five reasons why it's better to take a proactive approach to adaptation. The first is simply that adaptation takes time, and extreme weather events – like floods – often strike very quickly.

Secondly, it's usually cheaper to adapt a new building or project than it is to retro-fit an old one. If your climate change adaptation plan identifies flooding or hotter weather as a risk to your business, you may or may not consider it worthwhile to retro-fit your existing premises, but that information will help you to decide when and where you next move the business.

Thirdly, there may be immediate financial benefits to having a robust adaptation plan. Investors and insurance companies like to minimise risk, and an adaptation plan is one way to identify and minimise risk.

Fourthly, future legislative requirements may require you to produce an adaptation plan. The 2008 Climate Change Act gives the UK government the power to require organisations to report on how they're adapting to climate change. At present only 90 organisations – mainly utility and infrastructure operators like Network Rail – are required to report, but this number is likely to grow as the direct effects of climate change on business become more apparent.

Finally, identifying possible risks can help you to identify definite opportunities. Medical Photographic Services is a small Berkshire-based business that specialises in photographs of skin complaints that enable doctors to diagnose conditions remotely. Stronger sunlight and an extended holiday season in the UK are likely to lead to a rise in skin cancers caused by malignant melanomas. If diagnosed early, melanomas can be cured in 95 per cent of cases. Medical Photographic Services has designed an innovative product called Molemap to aid early diagnoses.

Impact on Business

The business impact of changing weather patterns falls into six main categories: logistics, buildings, people, processes, markets and finance.

LOGISTICS

Most businesses depend on road and rail for the transport of goods and people, and the UK's transport infrastructure is very vulnerable to weather-related disruption.

Rail is particularly vulnerable: high winds can knock out overhead power lines, hot weather can distort the rails resulting in speed restrictions, and flooding can render bridges unsafe and wash away whole sections of track. The only good news is that disruption caused by snow and ice that has been so prominent in the cold winters of 2009–2010 and 2010–2011 is likely to be diminished.

Roads are not immune. High winds can prevent high-sided vehicles using exposed motorways and river crossings. High temperatures result in a faster degradation of road surfaces. Flooding can stop all road transport in an area. During the 2009 floods in Cumbria, many homes and businesses could only be accessed by helicopter.

Although the 2011 Japanese tsunami wasn't caused by climate change, it illustrates the effect on an economy of widespread disruption due to flooding. Many Japanese manufacturers situated outside the affected area were badly hit by the failure of suppliers within it. Just in time manufacturing, pioneered by Toyota and now commonplace throughout the world, makes companies particularly vulnerable to interruptions in the supply chain.

Most businesses already have some kind of business continuity plan to prepare for disruptions to their supply chain; what these plans don't always acknowledge is that such disruptions are likely to become more frequent as a result of climate change.

Your other vulnerability as a business is to interruptions in your utility supplies: water, electricity, gas, phone and the Internet. The biggest power cut in recent times in the UK was in May 2007, when half a million people were left without power for 40 minutes. Operations were cancelled in High Wycombe hospital when its backup diesel generator failed, and eight people spent an uncomfortable hour in a stuck lift in Newcastle upon Tyne. Although this power outage was attributed to a huge coincidence of a number of power stations 'tripping out' at more or less the same time, it demonstrates the fragility of our electricity infrastructure. It's worth noting that the two of the biggest power cuts in history were both weather-related: when lightning struck a substation in São Paulo in 1999, the knock-on effects plunged almost 100 million Brazilians into darkness, and military police were put on the streets of Rio to prevent rioting; in 2003, an unusually hot day in Northern Ohio caused a single power cable to expand and sag into some trees, causing a short circuit that left 45 million Americans without power, phones or the Internet.

BUILDINGS

Increased winter precipitation coupled with a likely increase in extreme weather – especially winds – means that many buildings in the south of the UK may simply no longer be up to the job of keeping out the elements. Businesses based in England may be wise to consult the current building regulations for Scotland, which are designed with a more aggressive climate in mind.

Cooling offices, warehouses and factories in hotter summers will become more of an issue. There's no strict legal limit to how warm the workplace needs to be before employees can legitimately refuse to work – the legislation simply places an obligation to employers to provide a 'reasonable' working temperature. What feels reasonable to a human being depends on humidity, air movement, exposure time and the nature of the work, as well as absolute temperature. Nevertheless, providing a reasonable temperature is likely to become more difficult as mean temperatures rise and unusually high spikes become more common. In the period 1961–1990 London experienced an average 15 days a year when the temperature exceeded 25°C. According to research by UKCIP (the UK Climate Impact Programme, based at the University of Oxford), by 2040 London can expect more than 50 days a year when the temperature exceeds 25°C

Where your premises are located is also a key factor. Are you situated in a flood plain or in an area susceptible to rises in sea levels?

The effects of flooding are clear. The 2007 West Country floods affected 8,000 businesses and resulted in £1.5 billion of insurance claims. According to the Environment Agency, 5 million people in the UK live or work in premises at risk of flooding. Most vulnerable are low-lying coastal properties, susceptible to rising sea levels and storm surges. Nuclear power stations are usually built on the coast, as the sea provides a ready source of water for cooling, eliminating the need for the large cooling towers we associate with inland power stations. However, this makes them very vulnerable to flooding.

Adapting for climate change is an especially important consideration when considering new buildings. Will they be robust enough to stand up to more extreme weather? How can we control the temperature, especially as energy costs continue to rise? Where should they be located? These questions become especially critical for a building that is planned to last 50, 100 years or more, when the UK's climate will be very different from what it is now.

PEOPLE

The weather affects how people feel. High levels of humidity and precipitation adversely affect concentration (ask any teacher why a rainy Friday is always worse than a dry one), while sunshine reduces anxiety and scepticism. People generally don't function well if it's to hot or too cold, and warmer weather can lead to higher rates of hayfever and other allergic reactions, and higher rates of skin cancer. In times of extreme weather, employee concentration may decline if staff are worried about the effects of storms, floods and heatwaves on family and friends.

Perhaps more significantly, customer behaviours are affected by the weather. Food retailers have long known that different kinds of food sell better in different kinds of weather. Ice cream manufacturers couldn't keep up with demand in the hot summer of 2003, while Asda reported a surge in comfort foods like soup, custard and gravy during the cool, wet summer of 2008.

PROCESSES

Many business processes and activities are weather-dependent, but no industry is more vulnerable than agriculture. More than 60 per cent of the food we eat is grown in the UK, and many crops are highly dependent on both average and extreme temperatures and rainfall. To take just one example, blackcurrant yields have been falling steadily as a result of generally milder winters, and according to pharmaceutical giant GlaxoSmithKline (GSK), two varieties called Baldwin and Ben Lomond are on the point of extinction altogether. Why should GSK care? Because it buys 95 per cent of the UK's total blackcurrant crop for its best-selling Ribena drink. As part of the GSK climate adaptation plan, it's supporting research into new varieties of blackcurrant that will thrive in the warmer winters and hotter summers we expect in the decades ahead.

It's not just agricultural processes that are affected by climate change. Felixstowe is the UK's largest container port. Getting huge container ships in and out of the harbour has always been tricky in extreme weather, but that's not the key focus of the port's adaptation plans. It's things like investing in infrastructure: how strong does a crane have to be to operate in the high winds we can expect to see more frequently? As the ocean warms and tidal currents change, what kinds of dredging equipment are we going to need to keep the port open to increasingly larger vessels? The port's climate change adaptation plan has to take account of all these different factors.

MARKETS

While the effects of climate change on logistics, buildings, people and processes are mainly negative, the effect on markets can be very positive. The UK tourism industry will benefit from warmer, drier summers and a longer tourist season. Anyone providing goods or services to outdoor facilities, sports grounds, parks and beaches could see significant opportunities. The climate of southern England in the 2050s could be more like southern France today, with all the opportunities that this offers.

On the flip side, one industry that is set to suffer badly from climate change is skiing. The season in US and European ski resorts has already shortened by three weeks in the last forty years. According to the UK's Met Office, the amount of snow in the Scottish Highlands has been declining steadily for the last forty years, and despite the occasional cold winters in 2009 and 2010, this trend will continue. Alex Hill, chief government adviser with the Met Office, thinks it very unlikely that there will be a skiing industry at all in Scotland in fifty years' time. Some resorts are already diversifying in order to find alternative sources of income. For example, Cairngorm has built a funicular railway that operates throughout the year.

Civil construction companies are already benefiting from large infrastructure projects driven by climate change adaptation, especially in the area of flood defences and water supplies.

FINANCE

Insurance claims as a result of weather-related incidents have increased dramatically in recent years, and this has led to rising premiums. Some insurance companies may refuse cover altogether if they perceive your business to be inadequately prepared for climate change, while others will offer a reduced premium to those businesses which are seen to have been most effective at reducing risk.

Most businesses rely on banks for finance, and an assessment of risk has always been a significant part of banks' decision-making process when deciding whether to offer – or extend – a loan. How risky is this venture? What are the chances of something going wrong, and how serious are the consequences when they do? Increasingly, banks and other lenders will want to see evidence that you have properly assessed the climate change-related risks your business faces.

What Should You Do?

There are three steps to your climate change adaptation plan.

Firstly, assess the risks to your business under the six headings of logistics, buildings, people, processes, markets and finance. Larger businesses will have risk and business continuity functions that are responsible for this; smaller businesses may have to set up an ad hoc group to do so.

Once you've identified the risk, you can score it in terms of impact and likelihood. Assessing impact is usually quite straightforward – you know what the impact on your business would be if you had to do without electricity for a day, or if your staff refused to work because the warehouse was too hot. Assessing likelihood is much more difficult, given the uncertainties over climate change, but you should at least be able to grade something as unlikely, possible or probable over any given timescale.

Finally, you need to produce your adaptation plan, focusing your attention on those risks that are both high in impact and more likely to happen. The action you take will depend on the nature of the risk you identify. In some cases you'll want to take action now to reduce the likelihood of that risk occurring – installing air conditioning in the warehouse, for example. In other cases you might want to put in place some contingency plans – taking out a contract with a business continuity provider, who will agree to take incoming calls in the event of your main offices losing power for the day.

Adaptation in Practice

Kitley House Hotel is a historic country house located in an area of outstanding natural beauty near Plymouth in the South West of England. Climate change will affect the hotel in a number of ways. On the plus side, warmer summers will extend the tourist season and attract more visitors. On the minus side, climate change could affect travel arrangements – road and train travel has been badly affected in recent years, both by floods and heatwaves. The natural environment may be negatively impacted both by climate change itself and increased tourist numbers. The area is also at risk from drought as summers become warmer.

In 2009 proprietor Andrew Huckley took a number of actions. The hotel grounds have been re-landscaped, both to attract more wildlife and give better access to guests, including raised pathways beside water. A management system has increased water efficiency in the hotel, and new purchasing arrangements mean that more supplies are sourced locally, minimising travel costs and increasing security of supply in the event of transport disruption from extreme weather events.

Although the time and costs involved in adaptation measures provided a challenge to the hotel, the benefits are threefold: they save money in the short term, they enhance the customer proposition; and they enable the hotel's owners and staff to face the future with confidence.

14

The Sustainable Business

Sustainability is here to stay, or we may not be.
Niall Fitzgerald, UK CEO, Unilever

As we move towards a low-carbon economy, every business will have to take some action to manage energy, manage carbon and adapt to climate change. This is partly because government regulation will oblige you to do so, but mainly because it will cost you a great deal of money if you don't.

But in the early years of the twenty-first century, many businesses have gone much further: they're attempting to transform themselves into truly sustainable businesses. A 2008 survey of 150 chief executives of some of the world's largest companies identified five key challenges for business in the twenty-first century: capital funding, globalisation, the Internet, talent and sustainability.

What does is mean to be sustainable? While there's no precise definition of a sustainable organisation, any more than there's a precise definition of a green organisation, it's widely accepted that a sustainable enterprise meets the needs of the present without compromising the prospects of future generations. In practice, this means paying attention to five key areas: greenhouse gas emissions, scarce resources, waste, pollution and people. What do you have to do to be sustainable in each of these five areas?

Greenhouse Gas Emissions

Given that atmospheric levels of CO_2 and other greenhouse gases are already at a level that will cause the world to warm for some time to come, you could argue that the only way to avoid compromising the needs of future generations would be for your company to cease producing any greenhouse gas emissions at all.

This is, of course, totally unrealistic: even if you sourced all your energy from renewable sources and offset any other unavoidable greenhouse gas emissions to become operationally carbon-neutral, you would still be responsible for putting greenhouse gases into the atmosphere unless you could persuade all your suppliers and customers to do the same.

A much more realistic goal is to reduce your absolute levels of greenhouse gas emissions. Companies that can reduce their absolute levels of CO_2 emissions at least as rapidly as the UK's targets of 34 per cent reduction by 2020 and 80 per cent reduction by 2050 have a good claim to being sustainable. It's not that CO_2 and other greenhouse gases stay in the atmosphere for ever; they're absorbed by plants and oceans. The problem right now is that humans are putting greenhouse gases into the air much faster than plants and oceans can absorb them. Before the Industrial Revolution, human beings were still putting greenhouse gases into the air, especially methane from rice cultivation and livestock, and CO_2 from burning wood and coal. In pre-industrial times the quantities were small enough to be fully absorbed by plants and oceans. But since the Industrial Revolution got going and we started burning vast quantities of coal, and then oil and gas, mother nature hasn't been able to keep up. But if humans reduced their greenhouse gas emissions to 80 per cent of what they are now, many scientists believe that this would be enough to get the world back into equilibrium once more. It's perfectly feasible for most companies to reduce their CO_2 emissions by 34 per cent in less than ten years, and 80 per cent in less than forty.

Some organisations claim to be sustainable because they're reducing their carbon-intensity – their greenhouse gas emissions per unit of activity. While a reduction in carbon intensity is an admirable goal in itself, this doesn't make your organisation sustainable: if you're in a period of growth, your overall carbon emissions may be increasing even if your carbon-intensity is decreasing. This doesn't stop some companies claiming to be sustainable even though their emissions are actually rising. The term 'greenwash' is sometimes used to describe the actions taken by companies that wish to appear more sustainable than they are, and we'll return to this theme later in this chapter.

Scarce Resources

Becoming sustainable isn't just about reducing greenhouse gas emissions. It's also about the way your company uses other scarce resources. There are many scarce resources on the planet, including copper, silver, gold, palladium and platinum used in mobile phones, indium and gallium in solar PV panels, and cerium and lanthanum in cars. Companies that work in these areas are already taking steps to secure their supplies. In this section we'll focus on two key resources we tend to take for granted, but which are becoming increasingly scarce, with consequences for a whole range of businesses: water and wood.

WATER

The world is facing a global water crisis. The amount of water in the world is finite, but as the world population increases, and that population demands an ever higher material standard of living, our dependence on water means that more and more people will face shortages. According to the UN, a person needs a minimum of 50 litres a day for drinking, cooking, washing and sanitation. In 2010, roughly a billion of the world's inhabitants got by on less. The average European, meanwhile, uses 250–350 litres a day, depending on the country, and the average North American uses around 600 litres a day for his or her personal use. Seventy per cent of the world's water is not for personal use, but for agriculture. Producing 1 kilogram of cereal requires about 3,000 litres of water; 1 kilogram of beef needs more than 15,000 litres.

A third of the world's population already live in water-stressed countries, defined as countries where demand regularly outstrips supply. Some 60 per cent of China's 669 cities are short of water. In many parts of India, boreholes are depleting the water table faster than the annual rains can replenish it, resulting in water rationing in many big cities. During 2009 parts of Mumbai were receiving water for only 45 minutes a day and farmers faced reduced harvests from water-intensive rice crops. In the USA, the Colorado River, which provides water for most of the western United States, has dropped by 20 per cent over the last decade. Major cities, including Phoenix, Arizona and Las Vegas, Nevada, have implemented ambitious water conservation programmes.

According to the World Economic Forum, by 2030 more than half of the world's population will live in water-stressed areas, and the crisis of water bankruptcy may be the most serious short-term effect of climate change and increasing population.

In 2005 the southern Indian state of Kerala was in the middle of a three-year drought. Farmers were going out of business and families were suffering from severe water shortages. All the while, Coca-Cola's local bottling plant was operating at full capacity. The Coca-Cola Company uses a lot of water at its 900 bottling plants around the world – probably at least 10 litres of water for every litre of coke. Not only is this unsustainable in the long term, but in terms of reputation, it's very bad for company to be seen profiting while local communities suffer. In 2007 the company went into partnership with the environmental charity the World Wide Fund for Nature (WWF) in order to reduce its water usage, not only in its bottling plants, but throughout its supply chain. Coca-Cola is the world's biggest purchaser of sugar, another fairly water-intensive crop. As well as the eponymous sticky beverage, it also produces a range of fruit juices, and these are also water-intensive products. The company has also donated $20 million to a WWF project to protect the world's seven most critical freshwater basins, from the Danube in Europe to the Mekong in south-east Asia. The company hasn't yet reached its long-term goal of replenishing as much water as it takes, so it can't claim to be truly sustainable; but it has certainly made huge progress in that direction.

If your business uses a lot of water, or if you're located somewhere that has the potential to become water-stressed, you need to look carefully as what you can do both to reduce the overall amount of water you use and to secure supplies.

WOOD

Every day about 80,000 acres of rainforest are destroyed. In some cases the wood is used for timber or paper. In others the forest is simply cleared, sometimes by burning, in order to release the land for agricultural use. In Indonesia, for example, about 12,000 acres a day are destroyed, mainly in order to produce palm oil, a major ingredient in cosmetics and food products. Destroying rainforests is a very bad thing to do. Forests absorb a lot of CO_2. After the oceans, they're the biggest carbon sinks we have on the planet. The more you remove, the fewer there are to do the job. Worse still, when you chop or burn them, the CO_2 they've been storing for decades is instantly released into the atmosphere. That's why Indonesia, with a tiny industrial base, is the world's third largest emitter of greenhouse gases (after America and China): it's got a lot of forest, and it's destroying it quickly. Brazil is fourth, for the same reason. Globally, destroying rainforest probably accounts for a quarter of all greenhouse gas emissions – more than all the cars, trucks, boats and planes in the world put together. If you want your company to be sustainable, you'd better look at where your wood and paper comes from.

Fortunately, there are some agencies that will do the job for you. The Forest Stewardship Council (FSC) certifies wood imported into the UK, to ensure that it has been logged legally and from a sustainable source – that replacement trees have been planted, or the forest has been designed to regenerate naturally. Many British firms selling wood and wood-based products, including B&Q and Homebase, sell only FSC-certified products, and Warren Evans, the bed manufacturer mentioned in Chapter 13, was the first UK bed maker to source all its wood through the FSC.

As well as considering the front end of the product life cycle, low-carbon organisations must also consider the back end – the disposal of wood and paper products.

Each year about 5 million tonnes of paper are put into landfill in the UK, where it produces the greenhouse gas methane. This is completely unnecessary, as paper is easily recyclable. If you don't already have a system for recycling paper in your business, you need to set one up.

Although it's harder to recycle wood, it can be use to fuel a biomass power station. The UK's first commercial-scale biomass power station opened in 2007 on the Sembcorp industrial site near Middlesbrough in the North of England. It generates 30MW of electricity using a mixture of recycled wood (most of which would have gone to landfill) and specially grown wood from sustainably managed plantations.

Waste

Every year about 350 million tonnes of waste goes into landfill in the UK. That's bad, for three reasons.

Firstly, it takes up a lot of space, and on a crowded island, no one likes living or working too close to a rubbish tip. Secondly, as waste matter rots, it produces the greenhouse gas methane. In 2011 almost 3.5 per cent of the UK's total greenhouse gas emissions came from materials rotting in landfill sites. Thirdly, and worst of all, a huge amount of energy and resources are used to produce something that ends up being thrown away.

About a quarter of all waste is industrial, a by-product of manufacturing and construction.

Another major culprit is food. Each year in the UK about 20 per cent of all food produced is wasted, and most of that ends up in landfill – about 8 million tonnes a year.

On the global scale, a particular problem is plastic. In 2011 the world used 88 million barrels of oil every day, and 8 per cent of that – around 7 million barrels a day – goes into making plastic. Of the 300 million tonnes of plastic made each year, about half is used just once and thrown away. Around 500 billion plastic bags are produced each year, and they're in use for an average of 15 minutes before disposal. Some end up in landfill, some wash into the sea, and some degrade into toxins that enter the food chain – and eventually, us.

If you want to become a sustainable organisation, you have to reduce the amount of waste your company is responsible for, and there are four main strategies for doing that.

Firstly, you need to produce less waste in the first place. There's a long tradition in manufacturing of identifying and reducing waste. When Toyota invented its lean engineering system in the 1960s, one of its key aspects was the elimination of waste. There are a whole host of techniques associated with lean engineering that can help companies to eliminate waste.

Some of this is simple behavioural change, some of it involves product redesign, and some of it relies on new technologies. An interesting and potentially game-changing technology is the three-dimensional printer. Traditional manufacturing often involves taking a lump of something and cutting away the excess material until it's the required shape – an inherently wasteful process; 3D printing involves building something up in layers in a way that wastes hardly any raw material.

The second strategy for waste reduction is to get your customers to use products for longer. This is partly a question of product design, and partly a matter of changing the habits of your customers. Nearly half of all music players, digital cameras and TVs are thrown away while they're still working; a third of all clothing is disposed of when it's still perfectly wearable. According to WRAP, the Waste and Resources Action Programme, each year in the UK we could save almost £50 billion if we used items to the end of their working life instead of disposing of them part way through.

The third option is to make your products, or the components in them, recyclable.

Some plastic can be recycled. Polyethylene terephthalate, or PET, can easily be recycled, and in the USA, UK and across Europe, about a quarter of it already is. About half of all Coca-Cola bottles are made from PET. Not to be outdone, Pepsi announced in 2011 that it would be producing 100 per cent PET bottles made from plants rather than from oil.

The EU obliges car manufacturers to provide facilities for recycling cars at the end of their working lives, and car manufacturers are increasingly incorporating recycling considerations into the initial design. Xerox photocopiers are 97 per cent recyclable. If it's possible to do it with complex machines like cars and document imaging devices, it's possible to do with almost anything.

Although these three strategies can take you a long way towards reducing waste, attaining true sustainability may require a change in thinking – a new business model. Ian Cartwright is Chief Executive of Kingfisher, the group which owns the UK's largest chain of DIY stores, B&Q:

> We as retailers are examining how we might shift from selling items such as a power drill to selling the use of it, perhaps through leasing or fractional ownership.
> The other possibility is for us to redesign products in a cradle-to-cradle context, so that we run the whole recycling loop, making our value-add from controlling the component materials in the product rather than a one-time fire-and-forget sale.

In other words, the business model may move away from manufacturing a product that you forget about once you've sold it to a customer towards a model where you provide the customer with the benefits of that product through rental or some other mechanism. This already happens in some niche areas. Businesses rent photocopiers, and DIY enthusiasts rent specialist equipment like sanding machines. Increasing numbers of city dwellers rent cars on an hourly basis rather than buying them. There has always been a market for rental of high-end clothing, such as morning suits for weddings and specialist ballgowns. Increasingly, businesses are renting computing capacity in the cloud rather than purchasing their own servers. How could your business provide the benefits without selling the physical product?

Pollution

On 20 April 2010 the Deepwater Horizon drilling rig exploded, killing 11 of the 126 workers on board and releasing a flow of crude oil into the Bay of Mexico. The flow of oil continued unabated until 15 July, when a temporary cap reduced the flow. The well head was not completely sealed until September. The spillage of 5 million barrels of oil made it the worst in US history, affecting more than 300 miles of Louisiana coastline and destroying wildlife, tourism and the local fishing industry.

Pollution doesn't just occur when things go wrong. Many large businesses consistently produce waste substances that are harmful to people and to the environment. In the 1960s and 1970s, for example, industrial giant GE put more than 500 tonnes of toxic polychlorinated biphenyls (PCBs) into the Hudson River. Under the tenure of CEO Jack Welch, the company strenuously resisted any attempts to make it clean up the mess, until the US government forced it to do so.

Although it's easy to blame large industrial companies for pollution, every company is responsible for some pollution, at least if its employees ever travel anywhere by car. Although legislation has driven new technology and cleaner fuels to reduce the overall level of pollution, the average internal combustion engine-driven vehicle still emits CO_2, hydrocarbons, nitrogen oxides and particulates, all of which are harmful to the health of living things, including human beings – and that's quite apart from their contribution to climate change.

London has a particular problem. Every year since 2005 the city has violated EU clean air laws by exceeding the EU's 35-day allowance of high-pollution days. According to research in 2010, some 4,300 Londoners die prematurely every year as a result of exposure to small particulates from road vehicle exhaust.

As well as producing toxins as a result of your business processes, you may be putting toxic substances in your products themselves. Many cleaning products, paints and beauty products contain ingredients that are carcinogenic or disruptive of the human endocrine system. I once visited a factory that made dishwasher tablets, and was alarmed to find that the workers in the factory treated both the ingredients and the final tablets as highly toxic items, to be handled only with appropriate protective clothing. As consumers, we think nothing of handling them, and indeed eating off plates that have been exposed to them.

What's acceptable in products is constantly evolving. Lead was once commonplace in petrol and in paint, but was eventually banned once the health risks became clear. As information about products becomes more easily available, customers will become even more demanding about the safety of the ingredients and components in your products.

If you want your company to become sustainable, you must take a close look at the potentially harmful effects of pollutants released as a result of your company doing business.

People

In 2001, multi-billion-dollar sportswear company Nike admitted that it had employed children as young as ten to make shoes, clothing and footballs in Pakistan and Cambodia. In 2010, Apple hit the news over working conditions at one of its supplier's factories in southern China. According to the headlines, workers were treated so harshly at the Foxconn factory in Shenzhen that ten had killed themselves in the first half of the year. Working conditions in Foxconn are extremely tough. Workers typically work long hours for a £2.90 a day and sleep in cramped company dormitories. Discipline is rigidly enforced by company security officers.

Every organisation has an obligation to ensure that the people who make its products are treated fairly, even if they're employed by another company in another country. This isn't easy. As Nike pointed out in its first ever corporate responsibility report, issued in 2001 in the aftermath of the child labour controversy, it's one thing to tell your suppliers that they must employ only adults and treat them decently, but enforcing such standards the other side of the globe is quite a different matter. When contracting with suppliers, Nike had always insisted on strict age standards for employees, but in the late 1990s in Cambodia, fake evidence of age could be bought for $5. In Pakistan, extreme poverty meant the choice for many young girls was working in a factory or teenage prostitution.

In 2010, Apple was quick to point out that conditions in the Foxconn factory were typical of working conditions in many Chinese factories which supply goods to the West. The reality of global trade is that it's only possible to buy a T-shirt in the UK for a few pounds because someone in a factory on the other side of the world is working long hours for low pay. All organisations which source goods from abroad face this dilemma – to stay competitive in their home market means driving prices down, and this often means striking a very hard bargain with their suppliers. This is turn can mean that suppliers treat their workers pretty harshly – how harsh does this have to be to become unacceptable?

Although there are no easy answers to these questions, it's possible to address them. The UK's fourth largest pharmacy chain is part of the Co-operative Group. Like most pharmacies, much of its income is derived from selling unbranded generic drugs. Given the highly competitive nature of the high street pharmacy business, any pharmacy that could source its generic drugs more cheaply would give itself a big advantage. It was for this reason that the Co-operative Pharmacy decided to source some of its generic drugs from China. While manufacturing costs are much lower in China than in Europe and the USA, where many drugs are manufactured, the Co-op had concerns both about the quality and the working conditions. In order to address these concerns, the Co-operative Pharmacy decided on a joint venture in China – effectively creating its own factory there – rather than simply outsourcing to an existing manufacturer. The joint venture company, Tianjin Tasly Sants Pharmaceutical Company, is now supplying Co-operative Pharmacies across the UK from its £20 million state-of-the-art factory in the city of Tianjin, while providing fair wages and good working conditions for its employees.

Some organisations have embarked on fair trade agreements with their suppliers. This may mean paying suppliers above the market price. Marks & Spencer works with over 600 cotton farmers in the developing world to source material for its chinos, jeans and hoodies, while Sainsbury's sells fair trade chocolate and coffee alongside conventionally sourced brands. Only its bananas are 100 per cent fair trade. Coffee chain Starbucks sources 100 per cent of its coffee sold in the UK from fair trade sources.

Fair trade is also not uncontroversial. Without doubt it improves the working lives of the small-scale farmers in developing countries who participate in fair trade schemes. By definition, they receive more for their goods than they would if they'd sold at market rates. The critics of fair trade have two arguments: firstly, that suppliers sometimes benefit a little bit from fair trade, but not much – they still, on the whole, work long, gruelling hours for little recompense. In 2009 *The Financial Times* reported that some fair trade coffee farmers in Peru were being paid the equivalent of £2.20 a day – more than the market rate of £1.80, but not much better. The second criticism of fair trade is that is distorts the market, and that it creates dependency in poor farmers. Each year hundreds of thousands of people do earn their way out of poverty in the developing world, but they do so by engaging fully in the market economy, not by being protected from it.

If your business trades internationally, it will certainly be having an impact on the working lives of people in those countries. How much do you know about this impact? How much do you care? In the twentieth century, most people in the West knew very little about working conditions in other countries, and they cared even less about them. In the twenty-first century, people know a lot more, and they are becoming increasingly concerned about it. The Internet in all of its manifestations and cheap ways of accessing it – especially via smartphones – is making it easy for anyone to find out about the way your company treats its people at home and far away. This knowledge is increasingly influencing their buying decisions.

In the twenty-first century, no company is unaffected by sustainability concerns. Tiffany & Co. is the jewellery company made famous in the 1962 movie *Breakfast at Tiffany's*. For most of the company's 175-year history its customers didn't much care about where Tiffany's gold, silver and precious gems came from, and the company didn't either: it simply sourced the best quality it could find at a good price. During the 1990s, however, it became clear that not only were working conditions in (mainly African) gold mines dreadful, but that the proceeds of diamond sales were being used to fund civil wars in, among other places, Angola, Congo and Zimbabwe. Where did Tiffany's stand on this issue? The company made a decisive shift towards directly managing the whole process. They signed up to the No Dirty Gold campaign, which pushes for better mining conditions world wide, while switching all their gold and silver supplies to a single mine in Utah. As for diamonds, it complies with the Kimberley Process Certification Scheme, a multilateral agreement to restrict the trade in conflict diamonds.

Measurement and the Triple Bottom Line

Businesses have traditionally measured their success in financial terms. Although businesspeople like to talk about 'the bottom line', it's rarely a single number that tells you everything you need to know about the financial health of a business. Annual profit, share price, market capitalisation and return on capital all have something to say about how a business is performing financially.

If you want to create a sustainable organisation, financial measures alone are not enough. In 1994, John Elkington proposed that twenty-first-century businesses should have a triple bottom line – people, planet and profit. Profit is the traditional measure of business success. Whatever other priorities your business might have, you have to generate a certain amount of profit simply to stay in business. Planet is the measure that encompasses your business's environmental impact. It includes greenhouse gas emissions, use of scarce resources, waste and pollution. The exact measures will depend on your business – water is a big focus for Coca-Cola, while eliminating waste to landfill is the big issue for Xerox. People is the measure of your human capital, and would typically include information about working conditions and employee engagement, as well as your company's impact and involvement with local communities. Although the idea has an appealing simplicity, few companies have taken it up, possibly because it's hard to come up with a few numbers that incorporate all the elements of people, planet and profit you would wish to measure.

It's much more common to produce some kind of corporate sustainability report to complement the traditional annual report. The Co-operative Group, one of the UK's leading organisations when it comes to sustainability, produces an annual Group Sustainability Report. Under the heading 'Ecological Sustainability', it reports on progress with climate change, waste and packaging, biodiversity and toxins, while a section on 'Social Responsibility' details progress on fair trade, supplier capacity-building, animal welfare, ethical finance, social inclusion, diversity and community investment.

In the twentieth century these issues were peripheral to most businesses, and they were often tucked away under the heading of corporate social responsibility (CSR). The early years of the twenty-first century, however, saw many prominent business leaders making these core business issues. Terry Leahy, CEO of Britain's largest and most successful food retailer, said in 2007:

> *I am determined that Tesco should be a leader in helping to create a low-carbon economy. For Tesco this involves something much more than listing a series of environmentally friendly actions, although those do play their part. It demands that we transform our business model so that the reduction of our carbon footprint becomes a central business driver.*

Who Buys Sustainable Products?

In 2008, American researchers Environomics categorised Americans' attitude towards the environment and sustainability into three main segments: 21 per cent of all US citizens didn't care about the environment at all; 43 per cent were concerned about the environment, but were not strongly motivated to do anything about it, especially if this involved extra time or money. About half of this group were strongly motivated by religious principles and a belief that humans are superior to nature.

That left just 36 per cent who were concerned about the environment and who were willing to do something about it. A third of these – 12 per cent of the entire population – were what one might call 'committed greens'. They were willing to make serious financial and lifestyle choice sacrifices to protect the environment. The other two-thirds of this green group – 24 per cent of the entire population – did believe in protecting the environment, in order to preserve a healthy way of living for themselves and their families, but they were limited in their willingness to pay premium prices or go out of their way to do so.

While this research is based on Americans, studies in other countries have shown comparable results. In Russia the proportion of committed greens is lower, and in Germany it is higher, but the overall picture is similar. In summary, then, only around 1 in 8 of the population are willing to spend extra on a product or service that will protect the environment, but almost 8 out of 10 people will be attracted to a sustainable product, service or company if it involves no financial sacrifice or other inconvenience on their part.

It's these 8 out of 10 that make so many companies keen to promote their sustainability credentials, leading in some cases to what is known as greenwash – trying to appear more sustainable than you actually are. The biggest culprits are probably so-called beauty products that advertise themselves as natural, organic or environmentally friendly without any justification for doing so, and cars that claim to be fuel-efficient even though driving a typical car produces 12 times the greenhouse gas emissions as the equivalent journey by bus or coach, and 40 times the greenhouse gas emissions of a typical passenger train.

For this reason, some companies are quite reticent about proclaiming their green credentials. In 2006, clothing manufacturer Levi Strauss & Co. began sourcing some of its cotton organically. Although the amount was small –

about 2 per cent – a proportion was included in almost all of its jeans, so it could have announced that its jeans now contained some organic cotton, which it hoped to increase over the coming years. It didn't. The company quite rightly judged that a greenwashy announcement of that nature would have enraged activists and customers to demand that if organic cotton is such a good thing, all of Levi's jeans should be organic. Something similar had happened a few years earlier at Starbucks, which had claimed that fair trade coffee was available at all of its stores. Regular customers, encouraging each other through the Internet, began asking for fair trade coffee, only to discover that many stores couldn't keep the promise. To their credit, Starbucks owned up to its shortcomings and took action. In the UK and Ireland, all of Starbucks' coffee is now fair trade. Back at Levi's, the company was able to build its expertise in sourcing and working with organic cotton before it launched a range of 100 per cent organic jeans in 2007.

Why Create a Sustainable Business?

In the short run, being more sustainable costs money. Paying for renewable energy is more expensive than fossil fuel energy, recycling is sometimes more expensive than dumping waste into landfill, and paying a fair rate to workers in developing countries is more expensive than outsourcing to a low-cost Asian sweatshop. More generally, part of the reason material goods in the West have been so cheap is because consumers have until now not paid to reduce greenhouse gas emissions, pollution, waste or worker exploitation. If you have to pay for these things, it's likely that the price will go up in the short term.

But in the long term, it's often more cost-effective to be a sustainable business than not. Sustainable products often attract a premium price; saving energy, reducing waste and being more resource-efficient all reduce costs, and legislation, present and planned, will make a sustainable approach even more cost-effective.

Many companies strive to be sustainable because it's the right thing to do. When Charles Handy wrote an influential article in 2002 for *Harvard Business Review* called 'What's a Business For?', he reignited an age-old debate: do businesses exist simply to make money for shareholders, or are they there for some nobler purpose? Perhaps they have a broader responsibility to all of their stakeholders? Perhaps they even have a responsibility to future generations?

Responses to these questions change over time. In the latter years of the twentieth century, many businesspeople would have been proud to state that businesses exist simply to make money (though all kinds of other benefits flow from that premise). Since the 2008–2009 financial crisis, the pendulum seems to have swung the other way. More business leaders are seeing the role of business as providing some broader societal good, with money-making merely a subsidiary objective. An increasing number of businesses now see sustainability as a key business objective – according to a survey of 500 companies by the Carbon Disclosure Project, 68 per cent of businesses have sustainability embedded into their overall business strategy, and this includes major multinationals including Coca-Cola, Nestlé and Unilever. What's interesting is how they got there. In many cases multinational companies were attacked by green activists for destructive practices – Coca-Cola for using HFC refrigerant gases, Nestlé and Unilever for their use of palm oil, which leads to tropical rainforest destruction. Initial environmental actions in these companies were largely defensive, in order to protect their reputation. But as companies started to act in a more sustainable way, they not only found that it could be very profitable, they also discovered that this was something they really wanted to do.

Sustainability in Practice

Marks & Spencer is one of Britain's best-known retailers, with 700 stores in the UK, revenues of almost £10 billion and operating profits of around £800 million. In 2007, Chief Executive Stuart Rose launched Plan A, the company's commitment to sustainability, with ambitious targets for climate change, resource efficiency, waste, health and fair trade. Under each of these broad headings, the company has set a number of objectives. Climate change, for example, has four main objectives: to reduce operational carbon emissions by 35 per cent and make operations carbon-neutral; to help suppliers cut their carbon emissions, and to help customer reduce their carbon footprint.

Each objective is further subdivided into specific commitments, of which there are 179 in total. One of the carbon emissions commitments, for example, was to procure 100 per cent of its electricity from renewable energy.

In 2010 the company issued an interim Plan A report. How was it doing?

Store energy efficiency had improved by 23 per cent (per square foot of store space) and operational carbon emissions had reduced by 13 per cent; 54 per cent of all electricity was sourced from renewables, mainly through green tariffs, though some of this was sourced directly from small-scale generators, mainly hydro and wind. The company had also helped its employees to reduce their carbon footprint, for example by providing free energy meters to 38,000 staff and free loft insulation to 4,000 staff. The carbon footprint of many of its products had also been reduced, for example by establishing anaerobic digestion plants at some of its suppliers' farms, to generate electricity from waste. The long-term goal is to be a carbon-neutral company.

Water usage in food warehouses has been reduced by 62 per cent, but as the company admits, water usage in stores remains disappointing, with only an 8 per cent reduction since 2007; 76 per cent of all wood used in M&S products is from sustainable sources; 90 per cent of all fish sold in 2011 was sourced from sustainable sources, a big increase on 62 per cent the previous year. Waste from stores has been reduced by a third since the 2007 launch, and of the remaining waste, 94 per cent is recycled. The amount of (non-glass) packaging has been reduced by 46 per cent.

The main focus of the company's work on health has been to drive health and nutritional benefits across its food range, by reducing salt and fat content, and introducing better product labelling and health advice.

M&S set itself one key objective under the heading of fair trade: to ensure workforces and communities benefit in M&S's supply chain: 21 commitments underpin this objective, and by 2010, 12 had already been achieved, including continued expansion of fair trade food, including green beans from Kenya and wines from Chile. Eight commitments are on course, including supporting 15 ethical model factories in Bangladesh and India. One commitment is behind plan – its commitment to source 10 per cent of all cotton from fair trade sources.

Some of the company's most interesting Plan A initiatives fulfil a number of objectives simultaneously. In addition to donating around 300,000 damaged garments each year to Oxfam, customers who donate unwanted M&S clothing to Oxfam receive a £5 discount voucher to spend with Marks & Spencer. This reduces waste, encourages customers to act more sustainably, and supports Oxfam's work in developing countries.

15

Developing New Products

> *Business opportunities are like buses: there's always another one coming.*
>
> *Richard Branson, entrepreneur*

The biggest opportunities of all in the low-carbon economy arise from developing new products and services. In this chapter we'll consider what those opportunities might be, under the four headings of sustainability, low-carbon transport, energy efficiency and energy supply.

Sustainability

What kind of new sustainable products will consumers want as we move towards the low-carbon economy? In 2011, Sainsbury's and Unilever worked with consultancy Forum for the Future to consider what consumers might be looking for in 2020, and here are some of their conclusions.

Personal technology will play a big part. Apps on your mobile phone will check the origins of any product on sale, with information about its carbon footprint, the people who made it, and any health issues. Other devices might measure how healthily you're eating and how much carbon you're producing as you engage in various activities. Instead of cooling an entire fridge, why not have smart packaging that keeps food at exactly the right temperature in an ordinary cupboard? Increasingly common wireless devices will charge themselves with solar PV built into clothing or bags. Personalised products will become more common – soap with your own scent, or cereals made to order for your particular nutritional needs. Locally grown and sourced food will be more popular: instead of shopping at your local shop (which might source food from around the globe), you can have local food delivered to you. Local and regional goods exchanges will enable consumers to swap excess home-grown produce.

Although the report makes no claims that any of this will happen, the various scenarios it examines makes a convincing case that in general, technology will make it much easier for people to learn more about the sustainability of products, and to access them conveniently and cheaply. The challenge for any business is this: how would your customers feel if they knew all about the sustainability of your current products and services? If the answer is positive, what are you doing to promote those qualities? If the answer is negative, what action do you need to take now, as it's likely that those same customers will be finding out in the near future?

Of course, not all customers will choose a more sustainable product if the unsustainable one is cheaper, more convenient or more familiar. To what extent should companies only offer a sustainable product? Known as choice editing, there's a growing movement among sustainability practitioners that an organisation cannot truly claim to be sustainable if it offers any unsustainable products. In a 2011 survey of around 1,000 sustainability professionals, 78 per cent of respondents said that businesses have a duty to provide sustainable products instead of, rather than in addition to, unsustainable ones.

Low-carbon Transport

One of the most visible and dramatic changes we're likely to see in the switch to the low-carbon economy is the rise in electric vehicles. No one knows how quickly EVs will take the place of internal combustion engine vehicles, but the change, when it does come, may be quite abrupt. At some point within the next ten years it will be cheaper to buy and run an EV than an ICE vehicle. When this happens will depend on a number of factors: the price of oil, legislation around climate change and CO_2 emissions, government subsidies and preferential tax treatment for EVs, and above all, advances in battery technology. But happen it will. In 2010 there are only 5 cars for every 100 people in China, compared to 81 cars for every 100 people in the USA; 1.3 billion Chinese people want to own as many cars as the Americans, which is why the total number of cars on the planet it expected to double in less than thirty years. No one is predicting that anywhere near the amount of oil required for an ICE fleet is going to be available at any price, so a sizeable fleet of EVs worldwide seems almost certain.

All the world's major manufacturers are developing EVs. Even Rolls-Royce showcased an experimental electric Phantom at the 2011 Geneva Motor Show. In 2012, Renault/Nissan was the only major manufacturer selling mainstream electric vehicles, but other companies will enter the market over the next few years.

As sale of EVs increase, this will create opportunities for the suppliers of the major car firms. There will also be opportunities for servicing EVs. Above all, there will be opportunities for recharging the batteries. Brighton-based company Elektromotive manufactures and installs charging points for EVs. Founded in 2003, the company installed its first two Elektrobay charging points in London's Covent Garden in 2006. The company is now responsible for over 400 charging points in the UK, and sells charging points to 20 other countries.

THE RISE OF THE CAR CLUB

Why own a car if you can easily rent one just when you need it? The world's largest car-sharing network is Zipcar, with 650,000 members and 9,500 vehicles in the US, Canada and the UK. Members book a vehicle online and use a smartcard to access the vehicle. Smartphone users can do it all from their phone. They pay a fixed rate depending on how long they use the car for and how far they drive. The scheme has been very successful, and the model has now been replicated by a wide range of other organisations, including commercial competitors and even city councils. Cardiff City Council gives local residents the option of accessing a car for £5.20 an hour.

The Zipcar story highlights a key fact about low-carbon products generally: people will embrace them provided they're just as convenient, and just as cost-effective, as their high-carbon equivalents. From the first three years of its life, the company struggled to survive – so much so that the board brought in a new CEO, Scott Griffith, to replace founder Robin Chase. Griffith's key insight was to realise that while most members would walk five minutes from home to find a Zipcar, hardly ever could they be bothered to walk ten minutes or more. When the company chose to increase the density of its cars in fewer areas, demand really took off, making it one of the fastest-growing companies in the USA.

Not only is car club membership much cheaper than owning a car, it has a dramatic effect on CO_2 emissions. Motorists who have given up owning a car and joined a car club report that not only do they drive less, they drive in a more fuel-efficient manner. Car club membership is not quite as convenient as owning your own car, so it's easy to see why mileage decreases, but why drive more economically when you pay by time and distance, not fuel costs? Car club members responded by saying that renting a car made you much more aware of the real costs of motoring in a way that owning a vehicle makes it easy to ignore.

While many car club schemes use ICE or hybrid cars, the city of Paris runs a car club scheme based on electric cars. Parisians have the opportunity to hire a four-seater electric car with a range of 150 miles for about £8 an hour. The scheme is called Autolib, with a nod to the city's highly successful Vélib bike hire scheme. What's particularly interesting about the Autolib scheme is that the vehicles use a new kind of lithium polymer battery. Part of the reason the car's manufacturers Bolloré were keen to support the scheme is that it gives them an opportunity to test out the new batteries under realistic conditions.

Membership of car clubs in the UK has been increasing at 70 per cent a year for the last five years, and we're likely to see more ventures of this kind – and not only for cars. Businesses already hire photocopiers, and in some cases IT equipment, rather than buying them, and we are likely to see more companies offering the chance to rent equipment rather than purchasing it.

Energy Efficiency

If your company's products consume energy in use, there are opportunities to gain a competitive advantage by developing a more energy-efficient version of the standard product. In every area from airplanes to white goods to washing powder, energy efficiency is driving new product development.

When aircraft maker Boeing was deciding what its next generation of airplanes should look like, it asked 59 airlines that were potential customers to vote on what they wanted from a commercial aircraft – was it a plane that would travel 20 per cent faster, or a plane that would use 20 per cent less fuel. The vote was unanimous – the airlines wanted a more economical plane, and that vote led to the 787 which took to the air in 2009.

Since the EU introduced mandatory energy efficiency labelling of white goods and home appliances in 1995 there's been a steady improvement in the energy efficiency of such devices. In 2011 more than 95 per cent of all new dishwashers and 98 per cent of all washing machines are now rated A or A*.

In the intensely competitive washing powder market, Proctor & Gamble's Ariel took market share from Unilever's Persil by promoting its effectiveness at just 30°C; in 2006 its whole marketing campaign was based around the slogan 'turn to 30' with an explanation of the energy savings.

Whereas businesses usually monitor their energy bills quite closely, many domestic users don't, and this has created an interesting set of opportunities for simple energy monitoring equipment. The OWL electricity monitor is a simple low-cost device that allows householders to see exactly how much electricity they're using at any time, and the cumulative effect on electricity bills. AlertMe, based in Cambridge, produces a similar device that can display energy data on a computer. Users report that simply monitoring their energy usage reduces consumption by 10–20 per cent.

As well as producing more energy-efficient products, there are opportunities for reducing the energy usage of existing products. When the Mark Group was founded in 1974 as Mark Insulations, it was small family-run firm installing mainly loft and cavity wall insulation in the Leicester area. When local and national government began to subsidise domestic and commercial energy efficiency schemes, the company rapidly expanded its scope of operations, increasing staff in 2006 alone from some 400 employees to over 1,000. It operates across the UK – where it installs energy-saving measures in 6,000 homes each week – and has also expanded operations to the USA and Australia.

Harvard Engineering is a small manufacturing company based in Leeds, in the North of England. When originally founded by John McDonnell in 1993, it manufactured small control components for fluorescent lights. By the start of the twenty-first century it found itself increasingly competing with Philips and other large manufacturers. Innovation had always been a strong part of Harvard Engineering's culture, and in 2002 the firm's engineers came up with an innovative product called LeafNut. This enables local authorities to control the brightness of street lamps during the night, saving large amounts on their electricity bills. One of the first local authorities to install the system, Kirklees, saved £260,000 in its first year – a significant amount for a cash-strapped local authority.

PowerOasis was established in 2006 by former Motorola engineers Nick Smailes and Pete Bishop. Many mobile phone base stations are located far from any electricity grids, especially in developing countries, and the default solution is often to provide a diesel generator, regularly replenished from a road tanker. Although companies like Ericsson, which supplies network equipment to the telecom companies, have long been aware of the possibility of using renewable energy to power base stations, it was never seen as a very practical solution. Not only were the upfront costs much higher than the tried-and-tested diesel generator, both solar and wind power are variable and unreliable. PowerOasis provides a complete solution to manage an appropriate combination of renewable power, batteries and diesel which increases the quality and reliability of the power supply while reducing diesel and operational costs, often by 50 per cent or more. Revenue growth has risen by more than 300 per cent over the last two years.

Although many energy-saving products owe their success to an increasing desire on the part of customers to save money, in many cases customers are unaware of how much a particular product might be costing them – hence the success of energy monitoring devices like OWL and AlertMe, and hence the reason Proctor & Gamble had to explain to customers through its 'turn to 30' campaign that Ariel really would reduce their energy bills. In some cases, the market is driven not by customer demand, but by regulation.

There are in the world today about 6 billion mobile phone chargers and power adaptors for laptops and other devices, which convert high-voltage alternating current into low-voltage direct current. When first introduced, the conversion was done with a small transformer based on copper wires, which wasted more than half the power. A more energy-efficient solution existed in the form of an integrated circuit power adaptor, but this cost around 30 per cent more than the copper-based version. Since most consumers are unaware of the power involved in recharging their phone, there was no incentive to change. In 2002 the National Resources Defense Council, a US-based environmental action group with more than 1.3 million members, began campaigning for a change in regulation. In 2004 it succeeded in making integrated circuits mandatory for power adaptors in the USA, and so, effectively, throughout the world – few manufacturers want to make electronic equipment that cannot be sold in the USA. The reason your mobile phone charger is lighter than it used to be and no longer gets hot when it's plugged in is that it's now based on integrated circuits, not copper wires.

Energy Supply

The really big opportunities in the low-carbon economy will be in the area of energy supply. As we've seen, almost every country has ambitious targets for increasing its proportion of low-carbon energy, and governments are willing to give financial incentives to make that happen. In combination with increasing energy demand and rising prices for fossil fuels, it seems that renewable energy is bound to be full of opportunities. What makes it an even more enticing prospect is that unlike conventional power generation, which requires substantial ongoing fuel costs, renewable energy, when installed, is virtually free to run.

The two biggest opportunities are wind and solar. The amount of installed wind power is expected to double over the next three years, mainly from offshore generation. To date, only two large companies – Vesta and Siemens – have much of a track record in building turbines that are large enough and sturdy enough to withstand the harsh offshore environment, but a dozen or so other manufacturers are jostling to enter the market. The major US player in wind power is GE, which has already installed over 17,000 wind turbines worldwide, mainly in the 1.5–2.5MW range. It too is developing turbines for offshore, which tend to be much bigger and more powerful: 4MW is typical.

It's not only the turbines themselves which create opportunities, but the associated infrastructure, such as the jack-up barges needed to install and service offshore turbines, and the new power cables required to convey the power from where it's generated to where it's used.

The solar power industry is a bit different. There are scores of manufactures of solar PV cells – mainly in China – and thousands of companies that will install them. One of the UK's largest installers is Solarcentury, currently involved in a project to put more than 4,000 solar panels on the roof of the rebuilt Blackfriars Station in London. This will supply more than half of the station's total energy needs (not including, of course, powering the trains themselves).

Because solar and wind power is more expensive than conventional fossil fuel power, and not as predictable, it's still very dependent on government subsidies. When the UK government halved the Feed-in Tariff for solar PV in 2011, it put many small installers out of business. This is likely to be only a temporary setback – in some parts of the world renewables are already cheaper than fossil fuel power, and growth will be driven in these areas.

The biggest growth of all in wind and solar is likely to be in places that don't have easy access to a fossil-fuel-powered electricity grid. This is true in many parts of rural India and China. Other off-grid applications of solar PV include the US Army's use of it in Iraq and Afghanistan, in order to reduce the reliance on diesel generators which require fuel to be trucked through dangerous environments, small solar panels to power road signs in remote areas, and solar panels to power remote sensing equipment on oil pipelines.

One of the biggest and entirely unanticipated markets for early solar panels in California was illegal marijuana growers. The authorities had become skilled at spotting the location of illegal marijuana farms by the greatly increased power bills resulting from the lighting needed to nurture marijuana plants indoors. The dope growers responded by using solar panels to go off-grid.

Innovation in renewable technology will also provide opportunities. Most solar PV panels are based on crystalline silicon. This a technology that has been around since Bell Labs in New Jersey took a 1905 paper written by Albert Einstein on the photoelectric effect and used it to produce the world's first photovoltaic electricity in 1953. But an alternative technology called thin film technology (also sometimes known as CIGS, as it often uses copper, indium, gallium and selanide) is significantly cheaper to produce. US company First Solar will be using thin film technology in its project in the Chinese province of Inner Mongolia, where it will be building a solar farm covering nearly 25 square miles. When complete, the plant will deliver 2GW of power.

Shortly after the UK government announced that is was halving the solar PV FITs, it said that it was giving an additional £100 million to fund renewable energy in Scotland, and much of this money will go into the development of marine energy. One company that will benefit is Edinburgh-based Aquamarine Power. Although there's huge potential in wave power, no one has yet found a commercially viable way to harness it. This is what Aquamarine hopes to do. In essence, the concept is very simple: a kind of large metal flap is placed in shallow waters on the seabed. As the waves cause the flap to oscillate to and fro, it pumps high-pressure water to the shore, where a conventional generator turns the movement into electricity. While small pilot projects have been very promising, it requires a lot of money to design and build a version large enough and robust enough to be viable.

The aspect of innovation that offers the biggest prize is not energy production, but energy storage – batteries. In 2010 the US Department of Energy announced a $1.5 billion fund to develop and manufacture better batteries. Most EVs are powered by lithium ion batteries, which are themselves a huge advance on the nickel-metal hydride and lead acid batteries that preceded them in automotive applications. Lithium ion batteries have three serious disadvantages: they're expensive, heavy, and above all, take a long time to recharge. However, researchers at the University of Illinois have designed a battery which is a kind of hybrid of lithium ion and nickel hydride that can be fully recharged in just two minutes. Whether this technology will be the one to transform automotive batteries remains to be seen, but it seems highly likely that something will come along soon to make batteries cheaper, lighter and quicker to recharge, and when it does, the EV market, and associated opportunities, will grow very rapidly.

Not all the opportunities in 'clean tech', as the renewable energy business is often called, are high-tech or require large speculative investments. In 2012 the UK government announced that between 2014 and 2019, smart meters would be fitted to every household in the UK, at a total cost of about £10 billion. This will create lots of opportunities for manufacturers and installers.

The other major area of opportunity in clean energy is nuclear power. The problems at the Fukushima nuclear power plant following the Japanese tsunami have dampened enthusiasm for nuclear power in the Western world, but this will only be temporary. Desirable though truly renewable power is, it's hard to see how it can scale up quickly enough to replace coal- and gas-fired power stations. That huge solar farm covering 25 square miles of Inner Mongolia is rated at 2GW – less than the smallest of the 11 nuclear power stations currently under construction in China. There will also be great worldwide opportunities for the construction and running of nuclear power plants.

PART V
Making It Happen

The change towards a low-carbon economy presents opportunities and threats for your business. In order to grasp those opportunities and minimise the impact of the threats, you'll have to change your business – or even develop an entirely new one.

In Chapter 16 you'll learn how to transform an existing business to make it thrive in the low-carbon economy. Chapter 17 is about how to start a new enterprise – whether it's an entirely new business or the development of new products and services in an existing business. Finally, in Chapter 18, in the light of everything we've talked about so far, we'll consider what it means to be a leader in the low-carbon economy.

16

Transforming Your Business

The question is not whether we are able to change, but whether we are changing fast enough.

Angela Merkel, German Chancellor

Every organisation is different – it has its unique features, challenges and opportunities. But while every organisation is different, the principles of organisational change are pretty much the same – it's how you apply them that matters. Whether your organisation's large or small, whether you're the CEO or a newly appointed manager, you'll find the following seven steps a useful guide to transforming your organisation.

Make the Case for Change

If you want to bring about change in any organisation, you have to give people convincing answers to at least four major questions:

1. Why change?
2. What is the change?
3. Who will make it happen?
4. How will we make it happen?

By far the most important of these questions is the first one: 'Why change?' If people are convinced by the need to change, they'll find a way to make it happen, but if they can't see the point of change, they'll either ignore it or actively resist it. The reason most organisational change initiatives go wrong is because insufficient attention is devoted to answering the 'Why change?' question. That's why the first step in any change process – making the case for change – is the most critical.

How forcefully you need to make the case will depend on who you are, what you plan to do, and what kind of organisation you work for. If you're working in a small company facing rising energy bills, it will be fairly straightforward to persuade your boss to let you set up a small project to look at how you can reduce electricity consumption. On the other hand, if you're head of corporate sustainability at a large corporation and want to persuade your company to invest millions in becoming truly sustainable, you'll have a lot more persuading to do.

The five key reasons for changing your organisation are cost, regulation, reputation, engagement and doing the right thing. Which reasons you focus on depends very much on what you want to achieve.

If your initial focus is on managing energy, the two most powerful reasons for taking action are the rising costs of energy, and regulation in the form of government schemes like the CRC which make fossil fuel energy more expensive. You can often make a simple return on investment (ROI) argument: 'If we spend this much on energy efficiency, we'll save this much money.'

If your focus of attention is managing carbon, the ROI argument is more complicated. Measuring your carbon footprint will not directly lead to cost savings or additional revenues; if you choose to offset some of your greenhouse gas emissions, it will actually increase costs. But there are possible indirect financial benefits. Mapping out your greenhouse gas emissions throughout your supply chain can highlight cost-saving opportunities. Walkers Crisps reduced the cost of manufacturing when its carbon footprinting initiative highlighted the benefits of persuading farmers to reduce the moisture content of potatoes; Booth's supermarkets reduced refrigeration costs highlighted by the high greenhouse gas emissions of its older fridges. However, reputation can also be a strong argument for managing carbon. International train operator Eurostar is in direct competition with short-haul airlines, and being carbon-neutral gives it a competitive edge in the eyes of many of its actual and potential customers.

Persuading people to take action on climate change adaptation can be more difficult. Some investment of time and money is required, which may or may not produce an eventual financial return. In this instance, the best way to make the case is in terms of risk. In the same way that your company insures against fire, adaptation can be seen as an insurance against the more dramatically negative effects of climate change. People don't have to understand the intricacies of climate change or even believe that it is happening to be willing to take some adaptation measures – they simply need to understand that there's a risk of negative impacts from climate change that make it worth taking some defensive action.

If you want to create a sustainable organisation, you have a much bigger job of persuasion to do, and all five reasons for change – cost, regulation, reputation, engagement and doing the right thing – can be brought to bear.

Although most human beings like to think that they make decisions on a rational basis, the evidence points in the opposite direction – we actually make most decisions on the basis of feelings that are often far from rational. As a direct result of the 9/11 New York terrorist attacks in 2001, almost 3,000 people died. One of the side effects of this tragic event was that for a year afterwards, a lot of people who would have flown switched to driving instead. Even in normal times, driving feels a lot safer than flying, and with those terrible images of planes hitting skyscrapers firmly in people's brains, driving felt even more safe in comparison. Of course, although driving feels safer, it isn't – a regular traveller is more than 20 times more likely to die in a car than in a plane. As a result of this increase in long-distance road travel in the year after 9/11, an additional 1,500 people died who would not have done if they'd stuck with flying.

If you want to persuade people to take action, it's important to understand that rational argument alone is rarely enough. You must understand the ways in which decisions are taken irrationally. Three aspects of this are especially relevant to making the case for organisational change.

The first is what psychologists call the narrative fallacy, more commonly known as the power of stories. A single story is often more convincing that a whole mass of facts and figures. People will often believe the story, even when the facts and figures point in the opposite direction, hence the term narrative fallacy. How is this relevant to making the case for organisational change? Tell stories. Tell stories about the computers left on overnight in your offices, or the customers who took their trade elsewhere to a more sustainable competitor. Better still, bring those stories to life with vivid images – a photograph of your offices brightly lit at night while the surrounding buildings are in darkness will probably do more to create a willingness to save energy than a spreadsheet of energy bills.

The second way in which people are fairly consistently irrational is that they are highly risk-averse. Most people are more strongly motivated to hang on to what they've already got than they are by the prospect of gaining something new. But look at this another way – this means that people will go to great lengths to avoid losing something. Therefore, if you want to get people to take action, the argument 'If you do this, you'll benefit' is often less powerful than 'If you do nothing, you'll lose out.'

The strength of this approach was brought home to me in a conversation with a sustainability director of a large Plc who was having a tough time persuading his CEO to actively support the next stage of the sustainability programme. This director recounted to me how his CEO's eyes were glazing over as he listed the next stages in the proposed programme. Towards the end of his pitch, almost as an aside, the sustainability director mentioned that without this programme, the company would almost certainly drop below a major competitor in the following year's *Times* 100 greenest companies listing. At that point the CEO perked up. 'We can't let them beat us!' he said emphatically, and the programme was approved.

This brings us to a third way in which people are irrational decision-makers: they're highly influenced by peer pressure. This applies at every level in your organisation: the CEO will be influenced by what other CEOs are seen to do, and the people on the shop floor will be influenced by what their peers around them do.

This is not to say that you should be making the case for organisational change purely in emotional terms – it would be irresponsible to do so if there were not a strong rational case underpinning your argument. What I'm saying is that however strong the rational case, it's unlikely to get heard and acted upon unless you present it in a way that appeals to people's irrational and emotional sides.

Nowhere is this more true than in presenting the most powerful argument of all for creating a sustainable organisation: that it's simply the right thing to do. The rational case hinges on the facts of energy prices and the science of climate change: continuing the way we are now is not sustainable. But there is an emotional side to this as well.

At an organisational level, many companies make explicit statements of their values, which go beyond financial goals. Johnson & Johnson, the pharmaceutical and medical products company, articulates its corporate philosophy in its famous 'credo', first drafted by company founder Robert Wood Johnson in 1943. Although it's been regularly updated since then, the fundamental philosophy is patients first, then employees, then communities, and finally shareholders. More recently, many companies have articulated their values in a way that explicitly acknowledges environmental concerns. Making the case for sustainability in these companies is easier if it's seen to be part of what the organisations exist to do. As a new generation of leaders takes up senior roles in a wide range of organisations, we can expect to see more of this.

I began this section by emphasising the importance of answering the question 'Why change?' Not only do you need to answer this question for all the different people who will be involved in the change – from the senior managers who will authorise, support and resource it to the frontline staff who will actually make it happen – but you need to answer the question in such a way that it addresses people's real concern about change: 'What does this mean for me?'

It's relatively straightforward to explain why the organisation will benefit from a particular course of action, but it's often harder to explain how every individual involved will benefit personally. The more you're able to do this, the more successful your change initiative will be. This need to explain the individual benefits of change is often expressed by the acronym WIIFM – What's In It For Me? We often assume that people – including ourselves – are primarily motivated by external factors – money, status, recognition and so on. While these factors have a part to play, they're usually not the dominating factors in most jobs.

According to more than 25 years' research on what motivates people at work, external factors work best when the work is very routine and mundane. If the work requires any degree of thinking, judgement or creativity, external factors don't have much impact – they can even demotivate. What motivates people to do more creative work is the internal factors. People are different, but three internal motivators seem especially important – autonomy, mastery and purpose. Autonomy means being given some overall goal or direction, and then being left alone to get on with it. Mastery means spending a lot of time doing things you're good at, and having the opportunity to get even better. Purpose means doing work that you consider to be meaningful and worthwhile.

Create the Change Leadership Team

The biggest single mistake that change leaders make is spending insufficient time and effort on making the case for change. But running it a close second for the reason organisational change goes wrong is this: failure to have the right people leading the change.

If you try to make change happen by yourself, you'll almost certainly fail. As human beings, we have an ambiguous relationship with leaders: on the one hand we like strong leaders who can tell us what we have to do, and on the other we're deeply suspicious of people in power and their motives. If you have an extraordinarily charismatic personality, and a reputation for trustworthiness built up over a number of years, then maybe you can drive change on your own, but the rest us need to create some kind of change leadership team.

Whether this team is transforming a huge multinational organisation into a truly sustainable business or reducing the energy bills for a small or medium-size enterprise, its members must have three key qualities. Lacking these qualities, the change initiative will most likely fail.

The first is *commitment*. The people on the team must be completely committed to the change, whether it involves managing energy, managing carbon, adaptation, sustainability or developing new products. Why would you have people leading change who aren't fully committed to it? This can sometimes happen if people are allocated to a team because of their function, rather than their commitment: 'We'd better have someone from finance.' If there are members of the change leadership team who aren't fully committed, they should take steps to become more committed – perhaps by researching the reasons for the change in more detail – or leave the team.

The second quality, and perhaps the most important, is *credibility*. The people on the change leadership team must have credibility in the eyes of the people in the organisation they'll be influencing. The problem here is that the people with the most commitment sometimes don't have much credibility. I was once asked to advise an energy manager in a small company who was trying to encourage more of his colleagues to travel to work in environmentally friendly ways. During a green travel week, he had hoped that his example of cycling a round trip of more than 20 miles to and from work in a unseasonably wet weather would encourage his colleagues to forgo their cars, at least for the bus, and ideally for a bike. The initiative was a complete failure. Why? The energy manager had no credibility with his colleagues. Anyone who was crazy enough to cycle 20 miles in the rain was definitely not to be trusted on anything. This can be a problem when asking for volunteers to be 'green champions' in organisations. The people who are most enthusiastic about sustainability themselves may not have much credibility with their colleagues. My advice in the case of the cycling energy manager was to concentrate on understanding and enhancing his credibility across the organisation, while creating a different group of people to lead the work on green travel.

The third quality is *competence*. In addition to being committed and credible, the members of your change leadership need to be competent at leading organisational change. If they've been involved in leading change initiatives of any kind before, all well and good; if not, it may be appropriate to give them some kind of training or development in change leadership.

In his book *The Tipping Point*, Malcolm Gladwell explores the reason why change in societies, communities and businesses often seems to happen quite quickly. For a long time nothing seems to change, then quite suddenly the organisation reaches a tipping point and suddenly everything seems to change. According to Gladwell, you need three kinds of people to bring about this kind of change: he calls them mavens, salesmen and connectors. Mavens are subject matter experts – the people who really understand the topic inside out. Salesmen – I prefer the term persuaders – are people who are good at influencing others to take action. Connectors are people who know a lot of other people – they're the world's natural networkers.

When you put together a change leadership team, you need to include a good mixture of experts, persuaders and connectors. All too often organisations assume that the business unit's senior leadership team – the boss and his or her direct reports – is the right team to lead a change initiative. It usually isn't. Few senior leaders are really good at influence and persuasion – they're usually so used to telling people what to do that they never really learn the fairly subtle skills of influence. Few senior leaders are great connectors – because their day-to-day work usually involves working within their own department or specialist function, they rarely see the importance of networking across and beyond the organisation. In fact, the best networkers in many organisations are often to be found at fairly junior levels in the hierarchy – receptionists, personal assistants and the people who serve in the canteen.

The change leadership team needs a sponsor: a senior manager whose role is to agree what the team is there to do and ensure it has the resources to do it. Finding the right sponsor is critical to the success of the change leadership team, and to the success of the whole project. If the purpose of the team is to transform the entire organisation to becoming more sustainable, you probably need the CEO to be the sponsor. If the objective is more limited – to reduce energy costs in one department, for example – it's fine for a senior manager from that part of the business to take on the role.

Do the Research

Once you have the go-ahead for your project and put together a project team, the next stage is usually to do some research. There are often three aspects to this: internal facts and figures, internal culture and external benchmarking.

INTERNAL FACTS AND FIGURES

You need some good data about where your organisation is now. If you're working on energy efficiency, you need data on your electricity and other energy bills; if you're working on managing carbon, you need to find out what's currently known about your organisation's carbon footprint; if you're working on adaptation, you need to know what plans – if any – are already in place, and so on.

Sometimes it's very easy to access accurate, up-to-date, high-quality data. One of the reasons organisations often begin their sustainability journey by managing energy is that it's very easy to get data on electricity costs. If your company uses a significant amount of energy (more than roughly £500,000 a year), you'll already be enrolled in the government's CRC scheme, so you'll already have electricity meters that report on consumption every half hour. If you're a smaller company, it's cheap and easy to install computer-based systems that give you live information on energy consumption for your entire company or parts of it.

Sometimes it's more difficult to access the relevant data. If your goal is to increase your company's reputation for sustainability among its customers, you may have to commission some research to ask them what they think. Designing this research, and getting the right people to do it, is critical: what customers say about their current and future purchasing behaviour may not be an accurate reflection of what they actually do. Many consumers say that they would be willing to pay a premium price for a product that's sustainably produced, but when it comes to shelling out more at the checkout, they may behave differently.

INTERNAL CULTURE

If you're going to be successful at bringing about organisational change, you're going to have to understand how change happens in your organisation. Organisational cultures can be very different. In some organisations, formal authority counts for a lot: if you want something done, getting the bosses to issue an edict works very well. As one energy manager put it to me: 'In this organisation, if your manager asks you to jump, you jump ... and you ask how high on the way up!' In other organisations, formal authority counts for very little: teams and individuals have a great deal of autonomy. I once asked a middle manager at one such organisation who her boss was. She replied: 'I'm not really sure – it might be Simon or it might be Karen, but in any case, I don't see much of them. We tend to do our own thing in this department.'

Most organisations fall somewhere between these two extremes, but it's worth understanding how change really happens in your organisation. One useful technique is stakeholder analysis. For the change you want to bring about, list all the different groups of people who can influence this change or who'll be affected by it. For each group, and perhaps even for individuals within the group, list their attitude towards this change. Are they positive, neutral or hostile? How positive – lukewarm supporters, or raving enthusiasts? How hostile – slightly against the idea, or 'over my dead body'? Next, and most importantly, list the power and influence of each group and the individuals within it. Where does their influence lie on a scale from none to huge? Be particularly alert to those cases – common in most organisations – where a person's influence is out of all proportion to their place in the formal hierarchy: the senior manager who no one really takes any notice of, or the frontline worker who has a huge amount of influence.

The success or failure of your project will depend as much on your ability to work with and influence key stakeholders as it will on your rational analysis of the situation.

EXTERNAL BENCHMARKING

Finally, as part of the analysis stage, do some external benchmarking. Identify other organisations that have done relevant work in this area. You might choose other organisations to talk to because they have some similarities to your own organisation, or because they've done something particularly interesting in the topic you're focusing on, or simply because you have some good contacts through your existing networks.

External benchmarking is an especially useful way of raising expectations in your organisation of what's possible; remember that human beings are often influenced strongly by peer pressure. Your industry's trade association will probably be a good source of information on sustainability initiatives within your sector.

USING EXTERNAL EXPERTISE

It's often useful to bring in some external expertise to work with the change leadership team, and various options are available.

The Carbon Trust is a not-for-profit organisation that helps organisations in the UK prepare for the low-carbon economy. It was originally established by the UK government and funded in part by the Climate Change Levy – a small tax on all energy bills. Other countries have similar government-sponsored and funded organisations. When it was founded in 2001, the Carbon Trust provided many services to business for free or at a low cost. More recently, however, as demand for its services has increased and government funding has reduced, it's moved towards charging for its services at a market rate.

There are many consultancy firms offering services for the low-carbon economy. Some are specialist arms of more generic consultancies, while others focus entirely on the low-carbon economy. Some of these consultancies provide a wide range of services, from energy management to sustainability to new product development, while others focus on a particular aspect – carbon footprinting or adaptation, for example. My own company, 21st Century Leader, helps leaders to tackle sustainability issues within the broader context of twenty first century leadership.

Set a Goal

Once you've conducted the relevant research, you're ready to define the outcome of the change programme. What will it look like when it's done? Although becoming a truly sustainable organisation is a never-ending journey, it's vital to set clear, measurable goals for each stage of that journey.

Most organisations have some kind of change initiative happening most of the time. It's rare that at least some part of an organisation isn't involved in restructuring, cost-cutting, improving efficiency, becoming more customer-focused, becoming more innovative, or changing its culture. What's often missing – and this is the thing that really saps morale and induces lethargy – is knowing the end point of the change. Sometimes that's because the people leading the change don't really know themselves, and sometimes it's because they know, but haven't chosen to communicate it to everyone else. Either way, it's a disaster. Contrary to popular belief, human beings are incredibly adaptable to change. Few people live the same life over, year by year: relationships come and go, as do friends and family members, jobs change, the house and mortgage gets bigger or smaller, and so on. But what makes change bearable, and even exciting, is knowing what the end point will look like. To take a personal example, buying a house, at least in the UK, is usually a fairly nightmarish process – seemingly endless form-filling and bureaucracy, grappling with large sums of money, chivvying estate agents and solicitors, and at some point the sheer physical demands of packing up all one's possessions and unpacking them again somewhere else in a house decorated in someone else's taste. But what makes it all worthwhile is knowing that there's something positive at the end of the gruelling process.

Organisational change is not that dissimilar. People will put up with a lot of hard work and a lot of tough challenges if they believe that there's something positive at the end of it all. The key word here is *positive*. The driver for change is often negative: energy prices are rising; we're losing market share to a competitor with a better reputation; climate change is wrecking the planet. There's nothing wrong with this – in fact, most people are more strongly motivated by the prospect of avoiding bad things that they are by the prospect of achieving good things, so in terms of creating a motivation for change, the negatives work pretty well. But in order to sustain the hard work necessary to deliver that change, people need to know that there's an end point and it's something worthwhile and desirable – in short, it's something positive.

Articulating and communicating that positive end goal is the job of the change leadership team. Just how they do this depends on the scale of the change involved. If the end goal is nothing short of transforming the entire organisation, like Marks & Spencer's goal to be carbon-neutral by 2015, then this requires days, if not weeks, of work. You don't just pluck a goal like that out of thin air: you spend time analysing your own company's strengths and weaknesses, what your customers think of you, and what your competitors are up to. You think very carefully about how the world will change over the next five, ten or twenty years, perhaps using a technique like scenario planning, as explained in Part III of this book. What emerges from this process is a big, challenging goal, also sometimes called a vision. If this big goal excites people, you know it's probably the right one, and if it doesn't, it probably isn't.

Not every change programme requires this amount of effort. If you're simply aiming to reduce electricity consumption at one site, then the change management team can probably come up with its end goal in an hour or two. It simply takes a look at the numbers for current electricity consumption, discusses opportunities for energy efficiency, and comes up with a goal.

As well as coming up with the end goal of the change programme, it's also often very useful to give the change initiative a specific name. Marks & Spencer called its journey towards sustainability Plan A (because there is no plan B). It's not essential to brand your change programme in this way, but it's often a good idea to label what you're doing. If nothing else, it ensures that people know what they're involved in when they do something to help the change along.

How measurable should the end goal be? The short answer is that it should be as measurable as possible: if you can't measure the achievement of a goal, then you can't really say you've achieved it. However, it's not always that simple to set a measurable goal. Many companies wish to be carbon-neutral or sustainable, but as we have seen, it's not always easy to define exactly what that means. Carbon-neutral with or without offsetting? Sustainable with energy, carbon, water, raw materials, waste, or what? Although it's highly desirable to know right at the outset what you're aiming for, many companies have successfully transformed themselves on the basis of the end goal being something a little ill-defined, providing that the level of excitement about the goal compensates for a possible lack of clarity. One of the early tasks is to bring greater clarity to that end goal.

Design the Way Forward

Once you've researched where your company currently is and you've set a goal for where you want to be, you're ready to design the way forward.

Don't try to change everything in your organisation at once: focus on the areas where the least amount of effort will produce the most results. According to the Pareto Principle, also known at the 80/20 rule, in many situations 80 per cent of the effects derive from 20 per cent of the causes. The Pareto Principle is a rule of thumb, not an exact scientific formula: you may find that 86 per cent of your greenhouse gas emissions are produced by just 17 per cent of your company's functions, rather than a precise 80/20 split; nevertheless, the principle is extremely useful for identifying what some businesspeople like to call 'the low-hanging fruit' – the areas where the most impact will result from the least effort.

In most cases, the way forward will involve some changes in processes or equipment, along with some changes in people's behaviour.

PROCESSES AND EQUIPMENT

Most business processes are inherently inefficient. Simply taking a fresh look at them can lead to better practices. Much of the equipment you use in your business will have been designed and installed when energy usage and climate change were not a concern, and there are many opportunities for upgrading, adapting or replacing equipment.

CHANGING PEOPLE'S BEHAVIOUR

If you want to change people's behaviour, there are three factors you have to consider – their motivation, their capability, and the context in which they're working.

As we've seen, different people are motivated in different ways. Sometimes external motivation works. Cheltenham Borough Council found that it could reduce its energy costs by £3,000 per annum with a total investment of less than £50 in chocolates. Employees who remembered to turn their computers off at night found a single wrapped chocolate waiting for them the next day. This modest incentive not only encouraged more people to turn off their computers, but also created a conversation about energy usage and uses of council resources.

More often, internal motivation – especially the sense of doing something purposeful and worthwhile – is more powerful. Simply taking the time to explain to employees the current use of energy in your company and the implications, both for the short-term financial health of your company and the long-term consequences for climate change, can be the most powerful motivator of all.

However powerfully motivated people are to take action, they also need the capability – the skills and the knowledge – to actually take that action.

More powerful than individual motivation or capability is the power of context. Our behaviour is highly influenced by the behaviour of other people around us. To put it another way, people's behaviour is highly influenced by organisational culture. That's why an important early stage in any organisational change programme is to understand your organisation's culture.

Pilot the Change

Once you've analysed your research and designed some possible interventions, you're ready for some piloting.

It's almost always a good idea to pilot something before you roll it out throughout the whole of your organisation. However thoroughly you research an idea, you won't really know how good it is until you try it. Some of the biggest corporate catastrophes have occurred because organisations didn't test the idea properly first. It's also easier to persuade people to pilot something in just one part of your company than it is to persuade them to transform the entire organisation overnight.

When you pilot your new idea, there are two things you need to bear in mind.

Firstly, choose very carefully where you'll run the pilot. Ideally, you want to test it somewhere typical. It's tempting to try and test your idea with a sympathetic part of the business to show that it will work, but it's much better to run the pilot somewhere that's more typical of the organisation as a whole.

When Marks & Spencer wanted to pilot the manufacture of carbon-neutral clothing, it chose part of its bra range to test the concept. The supply chain of a bra is surprisingly complex, with 21 components from 12 different suppliers. M&S reckoned that if it could source carbon-neutral bras, it could source almost any kind of clothing in a carbon-neutral way. It probably also helped that M&S has a reputation for supplying a large proportion of the UK's underwear, so this made it a typical product to pilot. The pilot involved a substantial investment, including a new factory in Thulhiriya, Sri Lanka that produces less than a quarter of the carbon emissions of a typical factory. Carbon-neutrality is achieved by offsetting projects, also in Sri Lanka. This pilot has given M&S lots of useful information it can use as it attempts to source all of its products in a carbon-neutral way.

Secondly, be sure to extract all the learning from the pilot project. Although Marks & Spencer is known primarily for food and clothing, it does produce a small range of products for house and garden, and as part of its Plan A it decided to test out a few obviously green products. One of these was a wormery – a bin full of worms that turns kitchen waste into compost. It wasn't a success – when people want to buy worms, M&S is not the first place that springs to mind. The range was quickly dropped.

As part of its drive to reduce energy usage in stores, Co-operative Food decided to test putting sliding doors on all the fridges in a store in Manchester city centre. Although it knew that the doors would result in significant energy savings, there were concerns that customers would buy less frozen food simply because it was too much effort to open the doors. In fact, the doors had an unexpected effect on consumer behaviour: customers perceived the food to be 'fresher' because it was behind a glass door – an irrational response, but an interesting one.

Bear in mind also that the pilot is more likely to be successful because it's a pilot. When you pilot something, you take a lot of care to make sure that everyone involved is properly briefed and knows what's going to happen. When the pilot's running, it gets a lot of attention, and when people get a lot of attention, they tend to be on their best behaviour – the so-called Hawthorne Effect. For these reasons, pilots are more likely to be successful than the general roll-out, and you must take this into account when evaluating the learning from them.

Although the logical time to pilot a new idea is after the research and design stage and before full implementation, the great thing about pilots is that you can use them at any stage of the change process. In *Built to Last*, Jerry Porras and Jim Collins studied the characteristics of enduringly successful companies. One of the traits common to successful companies was a philosophy of 'try a lot of stuff and see what works'. Successful change involves lots of trial and error.

Implementation

Once you've piloted the idea and learned from that experience, you're ready to implement your ideas across the organisation. There are three things to bear in mind at this stage.

Firstly, some things that are easy to pilot may be difficult to roll out at scale. In 2006, Marks & Spencer piloted a range of fair trade clothing – mainly T-shirts and socks – at 40 of its stores. The cotton came from farmers in the Gujarat region of India who were paid a premium price in order to improve working conditions for their employees. The pilot was a great success, and the popularity of the range was reinforced by a survey commissioned by M&S which showed that a third of clothes shoppers were influenced in their buying decisions by concerns about the way products were sourced. In its 2011 sustainability report, however, the company admitted that despite being the world's largest retailer of fair trade clothing, it had struggled to source sustainable cotton and increase volumes significantly.

Secondly, implementing any kind of organisational change is hard work for the people involved. There's often a time lag between a new initiative and the results coming through, and it's easy for people to become cynical or disenchanted. Change expert Jim Collins has likened changing an organisation to starting a heavy flywheel turning: when it's spinning, it's easy to maintain momentum, but it takes a huge amount of effort to start it turning in the first place. Don't underestimate the effort involved in getting change going – and make sure that people understand the benefits.

Finally, external factors may affect what you're trying to do. Many organisations which were planning to install solar PV during 2011–2012 were thrown off course when the UK government abruptly announced that is was halving the Feed-in Tariff rates much earlier than expected.

Once you've overcome these obstacles and successfully implemented the new ways of working, it's time to consider what to do next. If you've tackled energy bills, you might want to have a look at transport; if you've sorted out your carbon footprint, it may be time to create a truly sustainable organisation.

17

Starting a New Enterprise

Your time is limited, so don't waste it living someone else's life. Don't be trapped by dogma – which is living with the results of other people's thinking. Don't let the noise of other's opinions drown out your own inner voice. And most important, have the courage to follow your heart and intuition.

Steve Jobs, CEO, Apple

Some of the biggest opportunities in the low-carbon economy are in developing new products and services. Sometimes you can do this within an existing business, and sometimes it's better to set up a completely new organisation. Whichever route you choose, there are some key issues to think about.

Where Are the Opportunities?

Broadly speaking, the low-carbon economy offers three kinds of opportunities. The first is a niche market for people who are prepared to pay a premium price for a product or service that is perceived to be green or sustainable. Organic and fair trade food and clothing, solvent-free paints, low-energy lighting, sustainable buildings, electric cars and renewable energy all currently fall into this category. Although these are niche areas, they can be very profitable, especially if they're presented and marketed in the right way. Many niche products will eventually become mainstream: LED and compact fluorescent lighting, once niche products, are rapidly becoming mainstream as costs come down and an increasing number of countries ban the sale of incandescent bulbs. It may take a little longer for electric cars to completely replace ICE vehicles, but it seems certain that they will do so at some point.

The second kind of opportunity is to be found with innovative products which meet a particular need for energy supply, energy efficiency, low-carbon transport or climate change adaptation. These products are not just green versions of an existing product; they do something completely new. Examples are renewable energy in all its forms, smart meters and energy-saving devices of all kinds, and electric cars.

The third kind of opportunity relates to the changes in working practices and lifestyle that result from the low-carbon economy. As more companies move to different forms of flexible and home-based working, both to save costs and reduce CO_2 emissions, there's a growing market for products that support this new way of working, especially in the area of technology and collaborative software.

As well as assessing the potential market, you must also look at the potential competition. If the product is innovative, you must protect your intellectual property.

Skills and Assets

There needs to be a good match between your skills and assets and the new products and services that you'll offer. The success of GE's Ecomagination initiative has been largely due to GE applying its existing engineering skills in areas like aircraft engines and electronics to things like wind turbines and more fuel-efficient railway locomotives.

Sometimes it's possible to use your physical assets in a new way. Gareth Williams runs 800 acres of farm in Herefordshire, and in 2010 he installed a 10kW solar panel on the roof of one of his farm buildings at a cost of £37,000. It generates about 10MWh of electricity each year, saving him around £1,000 a year in electricity costs. More significantly, through its system of Feed-in Tariffs, the government pays Gareth another £3,600 a year, index-linked, and guaranteed for the next 25 years. At current electricity prices, for an investment of £37,000, Gareth has secured himself an income of £4,600 a year. The panels pay for themselves in around eight years, and after that it's pure profit.

Just before he installed his solar PV, Gareth Williams also spent £52,000 on a 15kW wind turbine, which attracted Feed-in Tariffs, but at a lower rate than solar PV. Not only did the turbine produce less power than the solar panels, it's also broken down a few times. Gareth estimates the payback period from the turbine to be 86 years. Still, Gareth has learned from his experience and now runs a successful renewable energy business alongside his farm. It installs solar PV, solar thermal systems and heat pumps – but not wind turbines.

In addition to physical assets, you can build a new product on intangible assets like brand and reputation. Although retailers like Marks & Spencer, Sainsbury's and Tesco have no particular expertise in renewable energy, they all offer various renewable energy and energy efficiency services to their customers. Customers trust the brand.

If you're providing new products and services for an existing business, you need to consider to what extent a new product fits with your company's current offering. The Co-operative Group in the UK has long been a leader in sustainability and fair trade. This has been a great source of competitive advantage in its banking business. Many people are attracted to the Co-operative Bank because of its ethical stand and the fact that it refuses to invest in tobacco, arms and other dubious trades. There is a good fit between values and commerciality. There's not quite such a good fit in the food business, however. Although the Co-op is committed to fair trade, most of its retail outlets are small convenience stores, where typical customers care less about fair trade and more about convenience and price. This hasn't prevented the Co-op becoming one of the country's leading retailers of fair trade products, but it makes it a tougher business proposition.

Where's the Passion?

Starting a new business or launching a new product is tough. Around a third of all new businesses fail within the first three years, and new products tend to fail even quicker. Knowing that your skills and assets are a good match for the potential market isn't enough: you must also be passionate about it.

In 2004, three years after taking the helm at GE from the legendary Jack Welch, CEO Jeff Immelt proposed that GE reposition itself as a green company. After all, the company already had small businesses making solar panels and wind turbines. Given growing concerns about energy security and climate change, why not invest more heavily in clean technology and grow this part of the business? Immelt proposed to his top 35 executives that they invest $1.5 billion in a new GE business called Ecomagination. Of the 35 executives in the room, 5 thought the idea might be worth examining a bit more, and 30 were dead against it. The mood of the meeting was: 'We're an engineering company, not some fluffily alternative green enterprise.' At this point, Immelt's passion shone through: he could see in Ecomagination the opportunity both to make a significant difference to climate change and to make the company lots of money. He overruled his colleagues, and Ecomagination was launched the following year. Since that date, Ecomagination has delivered over $85 billion in revenues to GE, with revenue growth at twice the rate of other GE products.

Developing New Products

You can never be sure how customers will respond to a new product until you test it with them. However much market research you do, you will never know for sure until you try. Market research may even give you the wrong picture. Sony's market research in the 1970s showed no demand for a miniature tape player that couldn't record music, but the Walkman was one of the most successful products of its generation. More recently, there appeared little demand for a tablet computer without a keyboard until Apple launched the iPad in 2010 and sold 3 million units in 80 days.

If something's quite innovative, customers may not really understand it unless they can physically experience the product. As well as producing its signature all-electric sports car, Tesla also supplies batteries for the electric version of Daimler's Smart car. The deal nearly didn't happen: Daimler was initially reluctant to source batteries from a small company that seemed to be betting its future on a tiny niche market for high-performance sports cars. Tesla's Chief Technology Officer bought a petrol-driven Smart car in Mexico (they weren't then available in the USA), stripped out the engine and rebuilt it as an electric car powered by Tesla batteries. After Daimler's Head of Engineering drove the car for 15 minutes he was smitten, and a $50 million investment followed soon after.

The sooner you can test a prototype the better. Rolls-Royce isn't going into large-scale production of its electric Phantom just yet, but it has made one prototype which it is taking around the world to see how it's received by potential customers.

Testing can also enable you to make technical improvements to the product before full-scale roll-out. The idea of Aquamarine's wave power device is quite simple: a hinged flap anchored to the seabed pitches backwards and forwards in the waves, driving pumps which push high-pressure water along pipes to the shore. The pressurised water turns a generator which produces electricity.

To begin with, in 2004 the company tested two scale models in a water tank to prove the concept. Then in 2009 it built a full-size model and tested it in the sea over two winters for over 6,000 hours. As a result of these trials, further modifications were made to the device to improve power output, simplify installation and allow easier maintenance. In 2011 the first commercial device was installed in Orkney, to be followed by further devices in 2012 and 2013, providing 2.4MW of power. If these are successful, this could lead to large-scale roll-out of the concept, and installation at suitable sites in Scotland, Ireland and the west coast of America.

Testing allows you to discover all sorts of useful modifications to your product. When Philips first began selling compact fluorescent lightbulbs, it marketed the low-energy product as Earth Bulbs, a name which appealed to environmentalists, but no one else. When it renamed them Marathon Lamps, to emphasise the fact that they lasted more than six times longer than a conventional incandescent, sales rocketed.

What's the Business Model?

When you're developing a new business or a new product, it's easy to fall in the trap of assuming a traditional business model, which is something like this: design a product, manufacture it, and generate revenue by selling it to people who want to use it.

Many successful businesses challenge this assumption. Microsoft made its money not by manufacturing computers using its operating system, but by licensing other companies to install its operating system in their computers. Google makes its money not by charging customers to use its search engine, but by giving it away for free, and generating revenue from advertising. Apple makes plenty of money from the sale of hardware – computers, iPods, iPhones, iPads, but it's also the world's largest music retailer, with iTunes, and it also collects a 30 per cent royalty on every app sold in its online App Store. By creating its own ecosystem, Apple is able to generate multiple income streams.

What different business models might be appropriate in the low-carbon economy?

Some renewable energy companies offer free electricity for householders in return for installing solar PV panels on the roof. The company makes its money from government Feed-in Tariffs.

As the growth of Zipcar and other car club companies has shown, if you can make rental convenient enough, it will appeal just as much to some consumers as outright ownership. We're likely to see more rental schemes replacing ownership, possibly including batteries in electric vehicles.

We're not just moving towards a low-carbon economy, we're also moving towards a more globally connected economy. Transmission of information is virtually free. This has a big impact on business models. In the early part of the twentieth century, the traditional business model reigned supreme, and big companies tried to do everything: at one time the Ford motor company not only designed and manufactured cars, it also owned steel plants, mines and rubber plantations. Towards the end of the twentieth century, companies tended to focus on the things they were good at and outsource everything else: Nike, for example, has never owned any factories, preferring to outsource the making of its shoes while it concentrated on marketing and branding. Before the Internet came along, identifying the right business partners was often difficult, as Nike discovered to its cost when it was revealed that many of them were using illegal child labour. In the twenty-first century, however, the Internet makes it easy not only to discover potential business partners, but to work with them easily and effectively. For this reason, we're likely to see more products and services being delivered not by a single company, but by a number of different organisations, large and small, collaborating. Whether this is First Solar working with a Chinese partner on a 25 square mile solar farm or PowerOasis coming up with cheaper energy for Ericsson's remote telecommunications transmitters, businesses in the low-carbon economy will be all about networking, partnership and collaboration.

Funding

Any new product or business needs some kind of funding to cover the research and development that's necessary to turn an idea into a revenue-generating business. If you're lucky, you may be able to do that with your own funds. Elon Musk, the founder of Tesla Motors, initially put about $110 million of his own money into the company. He could afford to: as one of the co-founders of the PayPal online payment system, he pocketed a tidy sum when he sold that company to eBay.

For the rest of us, the options are bank loans, private investors, venture capital and government grants and loans. The mixture will depend on what you want to do.

The Torrs Hydro is a community-owned hydroelectric scheme at New Mills in Derbyshire. It generates 70kW of electricity which is supplied to local homes and businesses, including the local Co-operative foodstore. The cost of the scheme was financed by £165,000 of grant funding and a community share issue raising another £125,000.

Aquamarine is funded by three main shareholders: SSE Venture Capital, part of power company Scottish and Southern Energy, ABB, a power and automation company, and Scottish Enterprise, the Scottish government's enterprise agency. It has also received a number of loans, including a £3.4 million loan from Barclays to part-finance the completion of its 2.4MW wave power array in Orkney, and some outright grants, including $100,000 from the Oregon Wave Energy Trust to gather data on the wave power potential of the Northwest Pacific coast.

Launching a new product generally takes longer and costs more than you think, and it's essential to have a sound financing plan in place at the outset.

18

Leadership in the Low-carbon Economy

How could I look my grandchildren in the eye and say I knew what was happening to the world and did nothing?

David Attenborough, broadcaster

Do the Right Thing

Low-carbon leaders understand climate change. They know that climate change is a very serious long-term problem that requires action now.

Terry Leahy of Tesco:

We now know that the implications of climate change are huge. I am not a scientist. But I listen when the scientists say that, if we fail to mitigate climate change, the environmental, social and economic consequences will be stark and severe. This has profound implications for all of us, for our children, and for our children's children.

Lee Scott of Walmart:

I had embraced this idea that the world's climate is changing and that man played a part in that, and that Walmart can play a part in reducing man's impact. We recognized that Walmart had such a footprint in this world, and that we had a corresponding part to play in sustainability.

Low-carbon leaders understand sustainability. They understand that unlimited growth in consumption isn't possible when key resources are limited.

Justin King of Sainsbury's:

> *If we are to meet the sustainability challenges that lie ahead, it is important that companies such as Sainsbury's invest in the future right now. We do not see this plan as a luxury, it is rather, an essential investment that will ensure we can continue to provide customers with quality food at fair prices, sustainably.*

Elon Musk of Tesla Motors:

> *I think the biggest problem terrestrially that humanity faces is sustainable energy production and consumption.*

They've reached this conclusion through different routes. In some cases, it has been pressure from environmental activists that has pushed business leaders into examining the issues more closely.

In 1994 Ray Anderson was the chief executive of the biggest carpet tile maker on the planet, Interface. At 60 years of age, he was proud of his achievement in creating the company out of nothing when he'd quit his job at Milliken Carpet some twenty years earlier. The only thing that was bugging him was criticism from environmental groups and customers that his carpet tiles weren't very environmentally friendly: their production used a lot of nasty chemicals and produced a lot of nasty pollution. In order to understand what he was up against, he read the then recently published book by Paul Hawken, *The Ecology of Commerce*. It was the turning point. He decided to be part of the solution, not part of the problem. He set a goal – later described as 'Mission Zero' – for the company to be fully sustainable by 2020: no carbon emissions, no waste, no net usage of water. By 2007 the company was about halfway to its goal. Greenhouse gas emissions were down by 92 per cent, waste down and water usage down by 75 per cent. Not only that, but sales were up by two-thirds and profits had doubled. Ray Anderson died in 2011, and many obituaries described him as America's greenest businessman.

Low-carbon leaders understand that sustainability isn't just about physical resources; it's about people.

In the course of his work as a shoe designer, Sven Segal visited shoe factories in a number of developing countries. His first impression of any factory visit was the overpowering smell of glue, and the headaches it would give him.

Of course, factory workers were exposed to these fumes all day long. Witnessing deforestation in developing countries got him thinking about climate change. In 2006 Segal decided to quit his regular job and set up his own ethical shoe company, Po-Zu (Japanese for 'pause'). Beginning with ethically sourced and manufactured house slippers, the company now supplies to high street chains like John Lewis and Russell & Bromley.

Once you really understand what climate change is all about and what sustainability really means, you have a choice as a business leader. You can carry on doing business the way you currently do and try to ignore the fact that business as usual will in the long term have very serious negative consequences. Alternatively, you can do the right thing, which is to find a way to run your business sustainably – to maintain all the benefits a business currently brings, but with positive long-term consequences.

Engagement

Doing the right thing doesn't make you a leader; getting others to do the right thing does. You have to be able to engage people to take action.

If you want to get people to do something, the starting point is often to make the rational case for action. Low-carbon leaders do spend time explaining why it's important to reduce CO_2 emissions, use scarce resources wisely and treat people decently. But making a rational case isn't enough. Presentations full of bullet points, spreadsheets and policy documents might make a logical case for action, but they rarely engage people. To do that, you must appeal to people's emotions.

The most effective way to engage people emotionally is to tell stories. Muhammed Yunus is the founder and creator of the Grameen Bank, a microcredit institution that has helped 8.5 million Bangladeshi women out of poverty and spawned similar models around the world. He's a great storyteller, and this is his favourite story.

In 1974 Bangladesh was suffering from a famine that would eventually claim the lives of some 1.5 million people. As a young economics teacher at the University of Chittagong, Yunus wandered out one evening to a local village, where he struck up a conversation with a women called Sufia. Together with other families in the village, she was attempting to earn a frugal living by making and selling bamboo stools. Her business was failing because she couldn't borrow the money to buy raw materials. Yunus asked her how much money she needed. Sufia explained that she and the other 41 families in the village making bamboo furniture needed $27 to save their businesses – and the lives of their families.

'$27 each?' asked Yunus.

'No,' replied Sufia, 'Just $27 will be enough for all of us to buy the bamboo we need.'

Astonished that such a small sum could make such a large difference, Yunus offered to lend her the money there and then.

'When will we pay this back?' she asked. 'When you can afford to,' was the reply. The Grameen Bank concept was born.

Since then, the Grameen Bank has loaned over $7 billion, and helped more than 25 million Bangladeshi women escape from poverty. In 2006 it was the first commercial company to be awarded the Nobel Peace Prize, jointly with Yunus himself.

Even more powerful than creating stories is creating experiences. When John Elter was tasked with creating an entirely new kind of photocopier in the early 1990s, he wanted his team to have a deep appreciation of ecosystems. He took the team on two-day wilderness trips to examine at first hand how nature's ecosystems work together. Towards the end of the trip, not long after the team had seen a day dawn from the first glimmerings of light to the full brightness of the noon-day Sun, the group was led past a landfill site. Curious to examine it more closely in contrast to the undefiled nature they'd experienced, they found parts of an old Xerox copier. After two days in the wilderness, the insanity of filling the world with junk became clear, and for many team members that was a turning point in understanding Xerox's zero to landfill policy. Under the leadership of CEO Anne Mulcahy, Xerox has continued its drive to become more sustainable, with ambitious goals for waste, clean air and water, energy reduction, biodiversity and health.

Great stories and powerful experiences engage people in a way that dry facts and figures never can. But even great storytellers can fail to engage people in change if they fail to understand that communication is a two-way process.

Leaders who really engage people find a way to listen to what people have to say, to understand what people really want and need. Creating opportunities to listen to people is easy if you lead a small team – you just get together with them and start a conversation. It's much harder if you lead an organisation of thousands. It's all too easy to let your vision become entirely disconnected from the realities of the people in your organisation. Great leaders find a way to ensure that engagement is genuinely a two-way process.

CULTURE

Business leaders can influence others directly by rational arguments and by appealing to emotions through stories and other means, and they can influence people indirectly by creating a particular kind of organisational culture.

It's often assumed that the choices people make are down to their own personality and free will. While this plays a part, the biggest single influence on people's behaviour is the behaviour of other people around them – in business terms, the organisational culture. In a famous set of experiments in the 1960s, Solomon Asch asked for volunteers to be tested on their powers of perception. People were shown two lines of different lengths and asked to say which was the longest. In normal conditions, human beings come close to a 100 per cent success rate on such a simple task. But unknown to the volunteers, these were not normal conditions. Before the volunteer gave his or her opinion, five other people – apparently also volunteers, but actually in league with the experimenter – said that the shorter line was in fact the longer. In this situation, around a third of the volunteers agreed that the shorter line did indeed appear to them to be the longer.

If peer pressure can have such an impact in such a clear-cut case, imagine how powerful it is in more subtle situations, or when a person's exposed to a situation for much longer periods of time. The power of culture explains why people become involved in strange cults, why flared trousers look so strange to most of us now but seemed so right at the time, and why people's behaviour is often so different at work from what it is at home. Organisational culture matters: in *Built to Last*, one of the characteristics of the enduringly successful organisations studied by Jim Collins and Jerry Porras was 'cult-like cultures' – in other words, very strong organisational cultures that had a great influence on individual behaviour. If you want to change your organisation, you need to change the culture. How do you do that?

The most important thing to do is to role-model the kind of culture you want. If you want people to use less energy or produce less waste or recycle more or travel in a more environmentally friendly way, you have to role-model that yourself. You also have to get other influential people in the organisation to role-model that kind of behaviour too, and that sometimes means taking tough decisions about people who are unwilling to role-model the desired behaviour.

Role-modelling isn't easy. If senior business leaders want to role-model energy efficiency, it can be hard for them to give up huge offices, big cars and frequent flights. If they don't, it's an uphill struggle to get others to change their behaviour. But when they do, it can be very powerful indeed. And it's possible: Warren Buffett, until recently the richest man in the world (he gave most of it away to the Bill and Melinda Gates Foundation), still lives in the modest house in Omaha that he bought for $31,500 in 1958.

Role-modelling isn't the only way to change organisational culture – having the right systems and processes in place matters too. It's hard to promote paper recycling if you don't have separate bins for waste paper, for example. But having great systems won't make much difference if senior managers and other people of influence in the organisation don't use them.

The New World of Business

NEW WAYS OF WORKING

Having a job used to mean going to the same physical location, for a fixed working day, with a reasonable expectation of long-term job security. All this is changing. Technology has extended the working day beyond formal working hours – with email and smartphones, you can be contacted at any time. Technology has extended the range of places you can work – with a laptop and smartphone, you can work from home, while travelling or at a temporary 'hot desk'. Technology is destroying the conventional permanent job contract. More generally, we're seeing a move towards more project-based work. In a rapidly changing world, why give anyone a permanent job when you can almost certainly access the specific skills you need for a specific project more cheaply through the Internet?

While there will probably always be some job roles that require traditional ways of working, many do not. Driven partly by technology, partly by cost savings and partly by reduced CO_2 emissions, we're likely to see a continuing move towards this kind of flexible working. While there are many benefits, it can be harder to engage people when you are interacting with them remotely and for shorter periods. Apart from anything else, it's more difficult to build a relationship of trust when you never or rarely meet someone face to face. One of the biggest challenges for low-carbon leaders is how to win genuine commitment in a virtual world.

NEW BUSINESS MODELS

In 1995 Microsoft was already a large and profitable company, and its launch that year of Windows 95 looked set to secure its position as the dominant force in IT for decades. In that same year Microsoft put together a team of researchers, writers and project managers to produce a new encyclopaedia for the digital age – *Encarta*. Initially sold on CD-ROMs (remember them?), and later online, it was intended to add another major income stream to the Microsoft business empire.

The project flopped, and was finally abandoned by Microsoft in 2009. The reason? A better online encyclopaedia came along, driven by a completely different business model. In this business model the articles are researched and written for free, and the encyclopaedia itself is free to use. The organisation's fairly minimal running costs are covered by voluntary donations. The name of that organisation is Wikipedia.

Book publishing generally is seeing the emergence of many new business models. Traditional publishers still commission authors to write books, negotiate with printers to produce them, and with bookshops and libraries to stock them. But increasingly, authors, publishers and others are taking books straight to an online format, either as an ebook, an enhanced ebook or even as an app for a smartphone.

In every sector, new business models are challenging traditional approaches. Short-term car rental is challenging traditional car ownership, especially for people who live in cities. Battery-swapping schemes may replace battery ownership as the business model for powering electric vehicles. If you think Wikipedia's free business model applies only to online businesses, what about companies that will install solar panels on your roof for free, and let you have the free electricity they generate, while they take their profits from Feed-in Tariffs? Looking further ahead, it's not inconceivable that electricity suppliers may let you have free electricity to charge up your electric car at night if you agree to let them have some of that power back again during the day, when demand is highest.

In the same way as no one would have guessed in 1995 that Wikipedia's business model for an encyclopaedia would triumph over Microsoft's for *Encarta*, it's impossible to predict which business models will triumph in which sectors as we move further into the low-carbon economy. But we can be certain that many new business models will succeed, and leaders in the low-carbon economy need to understand and be familiar with them.

NEW PARTNERSHIPS

As organisations search for the best way to find the skills needed to deliver a particular project, we're seeing not only more partnership work, but more unexpected partners. When the Coca-Cola Company formed a partnership with the not-for-profit WWF, it perceived a risk on both sides. What would the shareholders of a profit-driven global brand like Coca-Cola think about cosying up with an environmental campaigning organisation like WWF? Worse still for WWF, would its supporters feel that it had sold out by working with the world's most successful purveyor of flavoured water? In reality, the partnership makes sense. Only by working together do they have the skills and influence to reduce Coca-Cola's water usage, with beneficial effects both for Coca-Cola's reputation and profitability and for the environment which it is WWF's mission to protect. Marcia Marsh is WWF's Chief Operating Officer in the USA:

> Working alone, NGOs are simply unable to reverse the tide of global change. To do this, we have to develop new partnerships with businesses and governments, partnerships whose scale of impact is commensurate with the problems we face.

A number of large businesses are finding it useful to work with not-for-profit organisations on their sustainability strategy. Forum for the Future, a not-for-profit organisation, works closely with Sainsbury's, Kingfisher, BT, Shell, Unilever and other large corporates on their sustainability strategies.

An interesting trend over recent years has been partnerships and acquisitions between companies with seemingly different value bases. Innocent Smoothies – famous for wholesome ingredients, ethical sourcing and donating 10 per cent of all profits to charitable causes – is now 58 per cent owned by Coca-Cola.

Body Shop, the ethical cosmetics company founded by Anita Roddick, is now owned by L'Oréal.

The Big Challenge for Low-carbon Leaders

Low-carbon leaders understand the issues of climate change and sustainability well enough to know the right thing to do. In some cases doing the right thing can enhance profitability – the most obvious example being energy efficiency. Less energy usage means less CO_2 emissions, which is good for the planet, and lower energy bills, which is good for the bottom line. Reducing waste is similarly beneficial to the planet and to profits.

The further you move towards being truly sustainable, however, the more the conflict between sustainability and profit becomes apparent. Patio heaters are not a particularly sustainable product, and in 2007 Wyvale Garden Centres decided to stop selling them. B&Q, part of the Kingfisher Group, followed suit a year later. In both cases it made a small dent in the company's profits: other retailers – including Tesco – continue to sell them. Who has made the right call? On the one hand, patio heaters would not feature in anybody's version of a sustainable world; on the other hand, if Wyvale, B&Q and Tesco stopped selling all of their currently unsustainable products, their businesses would cease to exist overnight.

For low-carbon leaders, this is the biggest challenge of all: how can you move your company towards a more sustainable model, while at the same time continuing to generate enough cash to function as a viable business – even if this means being unsustainable in the short and medium term. This is a particularly tough call when it comes to the people side of sustainability. Tesco in the UK and Walmart in the USA have both had a huge impact on good practice in sustainability, in terms of influencing their own suppliers, customers and employees as well as setting a standard for other businesses. As the influential US not-for-profit Environmental Defense Fund commented: 'Leadership on environmental issues is coming from Bentonville [Walmart's HQ] these days, not from Washington.'

On the other hand, both Tesco and Walmart have both been criticised for harming local communities with their 'big box' model of retailing and their aggressive stance towards suppliers. It's the economies of scale that result from big superstores and driving a tough bargain with suppliers that enable

Tesco and Walmart to generate the profits to invest in their sustainability initiatives.

Or is it? In *Firms of Endearment*, Raj Sisodia, Jag Seth and David Wolfe report on their research into 28 firms which strive to meet the needs of all stakeholders, including local communities and suppliers. These firms are often thought of with great affection by their customers, employees, suppliers, owners and the communities in which they operate – hence the name 'firms of endearment'. These firms of endearment were very profitable. Over a ten-year period from 1996 to 2006, the average returns on publicly traded shares of firms of endearment were eight times more profitable than the general market, so perhaps a broader stakeholder approach can go hand in hand with financial success.

There are no easy answers to this conundrum. While it's true that some sustainability initiatives can generate additional profits, it's also true that moving too quickly to a fully sustainable model would destroy them – which is why even the most ardent advocates of sustainability, like Ray Anderson at Interface, think in terms of years and decades, not months. Move too quickly towards sustainability, and you wreck the business. Move too slowly, and you wreck the planet, together with the prospects of the people who live on it. Getting the pace of change just right is the biggest challenge facing business leaders today.

Bibliography

Berners-Lee, Mike (2010) *How Bad Are Bananas?*, London: Profile Books.

Booker, Christopher (2009) *The Real Global Warming Disaster*, London: Continuum.

Bower, Tom (2009) *The Squeeze: Oil, Money and Greed in the 21st Century*, London: Harper.

Brand, Stewart (2009) *Whole Earth Discipline*, London: Atlantic.

Chamberlain, Shaun (2009) *The Transition Timeline*, Dartington: Green Books.

Collins, Jim (2001) *Good to Great*, London: Random House.

Collins, Jim and Porras, Jerry (1996) *Built to Last*, London: Century.

Diamond, Jared (2005) *Collapse*, London: Penguin.

Downey, Morgan (2009) *Oil 101*, London: Wooden Table.

Dyer, Gwynne (2010) *Climate Wars*, Oxford: Oneworld.

Elkington, John (1997) *Cannibals with Forks*, Oxford: Capstone.

Estes, Jonathan (2009) *Smart Green*, Hoboken, NJ: John Wiley.

Esty, Daniel and Winston, Andrew (2006) *Green to Gold*, Hoboken, NJ: John Wiley.

Fetzer, Amy and Aaron, Shari (2010) *Climb the Green Ladder*, Hoboken, NJ: John Wiley.

Flannery, Tim (2005) *The Weather Makers*, London: Penguin.

Friedman, Tom (2009) *Hot, Flat and Crowded*, London, Penguin.

Friedman, Tom (2011) *That Used to Be Us*, London, Penguin.

Gardner, Daniel (2011) *Future Babble*, London: Virgin.

Giddens, Anthony (2009) *The Politics of Climate Change*, Cambridge: Polity Press.

Gladwell, Malcolm (2000) *The Tipping Point*, London: Penguin.

Goleman, Daniel (2009) *Ecological Intelligence*, London: Allen Lane.

Goodall, Chris (2009) *The Green Guide for Business*, London: Profile Books.

Gratton, Lynda (2011) *The Shift: The Future of Work is Already Here*, London: Collins.

Hansen, James (2009) *Storms of my Grandchildren*, London: Bloomsbury.

Hawken, Paul (1993) *The Ecology of Commerce*, New York: Harper.

Heinberg, Richard (2003) *The Party's Over*, Forest Row: Clairview.

Henson, Robert (2008) *The Rough Guide to Climate Change*, London: Rough Guides.

Hofmeister, John (2010) *Why We Hate the Oil Companies*, New York: Palgrave Macmillan.

Holmgren, David (2009) *Future Scenarios*, Dartington: Green Books.

Hopkins, Rob (2008) *The Transition Handbook*, Dartington: Green Books.

Jackson, Tim (2009) *Prosperity Without Growth*, London: Earthscan.

Jolly, Adam (2010) *Clean Tech, Clean Profits*, London: Kogan Page.

Kane, Gareth (2010) *The Three Secrets of Green Business*, London: Earthscan.

Kane, Gareth (2011) *The Green Executive*, London: Earthscan.

Kiernan, Matthew (2009) *Investing in a Sustainable World*, New York: Amacom.

Kohn, Marek (2010) *Turned Out Nice*, London: Faber and Faber.

Kotter, John (1996) *Leading Change*, Boston, MA: Harvard Business School.

Kunzig, Robert and Broecker, Wallace (2008) *Fixing Climate*, London: Profile Books.

Lawson, Nigel (2008) *An Appeal to Reason: A Cool Look at Global Warming*, London: Duckworth Overlook.

Layard, Richard, *Happiness*, London: Penguin.

Lepsinger, Richard (2010) *Virtual Team Success*, San Francisco, CA: Jossey-Bass.

Little, Amanda (2009) *Power Trip*, London: Harper Press.

Lomberg, Bjørn (2007) *Cool It: The Skeptical Environmentalist's Guide to Global Warming*, London: Marshall Cavendish.

Lomberg, Bjørn (2010) *Smart Solutions to Climate Change*, Cambridge: Cambridge University Press.

Lynas, Mark (2007) *Six Degrees*, London: Harper Perennial.

MacKay, David (2009) *Sustainable Energy Without the Hot Air*, Cambridge: UIT Cambridge.

Makower, Joel (2009) *Strategies for the Green Economy*, New York: McGraw-Hill.

McKibben, Bill (2007) *Deep Economy*, Oxford: Oneworld Publications.

Monbiot, George (2006) *Heat*, London: Penguin.

Osterwald, Alexander and Pigneur, Yves (2010) *Business Model Generation*, Hoboken, NJ: John Wiley.

Pernick, Ron and Wilder, Clint (2008) *The Clean Tech Revolution*, New York: Collins Business.

Pielke, Roger (2010) *The Climate Fix*, New York: Basic Books.

Pink, Daniel (2010) *Drive*, Edinburgh: Canongate.

Ridley, Matt (2010) *The Rational Optimist*, London: Fourth Estate.

Rogers, Heather (2010) *Green Gone Wrong*, London: Verso.

Rubin, Jeff (2009) *Why Your World is About to Get a Whole Lot Smaller*, London: Virgin.

Savitz, Andrew (2006) *The Triple Bottom Line*, San Francisco, CA: Jossey-Bass.

Senge, Peter (2008) *The Necessary Revolution*, London: Nicholas Brealey.

Simmons, Matthew (2005) *Twilight in the Desert*, Hoboken, NJ: John Wiley.

Sisodia, Raj, Sheth, Jag and Wolfe, David (2007) *Firms of Endearment*, Upper Saddle River, NJ: Wharton.

Sperling, Daniel and Gordon, Deborah (2009) *Two Billion Cars*, Oxford: Oxford University Press.

Tappin, Steve and Cave, Andrew (2008) *The Secrets of CEOs*, London, Nicholas Brealey.

Weightman, Gavin (2011) *Children of Light*, London: Atlantic Books.

Werbach, Adam (2009) *Strategy for Sustainability*, Boston, MA: Harvard Business Press.

Wilkinson, Richard and Pickett, Kate (2009) *The Spirit Level*, London: Penguin.

Yergin, Daniel (1991) *The Prize*, London: Simon and Schuster.

Yergin, Daniel (2011) *The Quest: Energy, Security and the Remaking of the Modern World*, London: Penguin.

Yunus, Muhammad (2008) *Creating a World Without Poverty*, New York: Public Affairs.

Index

If you have found this book useful you may be interested in other titles from Gower

**Design for Sustainability
A Practical Approach**
Tracy Bhamra and Vicky Lofthouse
Hardback: 978-0-566-08704-2
Ebook: 978-0-7546-8775-7

**Energy, Environment, Natural Resources and
Business Competitiveness
The Fragility of Interdependence**
Dimitris N. Chorafas
Hardback: 978-0-566-09234-3
Ebook: 978-0-566-09235-0

**Longer Lasting Products
Alternatives To The Throwaway Society**
Edited by Tim Cooper
Hardback: 978-0-566-08808-7
Ebook: 978-1-4094-1043-0

**Plan for the Planet
A Business Plan for a Sustainable World**
Ian Chambers and John Humble
Paperback: 978-1-4094-4589-0
Ebook: 978-1-4094-0682-2

GOWER

**Green Outcomes in the Real World
Global Forces, Local Circumstances, and
Sustainable Solutions**
Peter McManners
Hardback: 978-0-566-09179-7
Ebook: 978-0-566-09180-3

**No Waste
Managing Sustainability in Construction**
Uly Ma
Hardback: 978-0-566-08803-2
Ebook: 978-1-4094-3646-1

**Sustainable Growth in a Post-Scarcity World
Consumption, Demand, and the Poverty Penalty**
Philip Sadler
Hardback: 978-0-566-09158-2
Ebook: 978-0-566-09159-9

**Towards Ecological Taxation
The Efficacy of Emissions-Related Motor Taxation**
David Russell
Hardback: 978-0-566-08979-4
Ebook: 978-0-566-08980-0

Visit **www.gowerpublishing.com** and

- search the entire catalogue of Gower books in print
- order titles online at 10% discount
- take advantage of special offers
- sign up for our monthly e-mail update service
- download free sample chapters from all recent titles
- download or order our catalogue